The Mystical Doctrine of St John of the Cross

The Mystical Doctrine of St John of the Cross

Selected by R. H. J. Steuart

Sheed and Ward
London

INTRODUCTION

By R. H. J. Steuart, S.J.

The question which divides opinion on the subject of the contemplative vocation is whether God calls to it all who desire it, or whether the call is a limited one, affecting only a relatively small number, so that without it no effort or aspiration is of any avail. The answer to this question has commonly been thought to be supplied by St. John of the Cross in *The Dark Night* (Bk. I., Chapter IX.), where he says that " God does not raise to contemplation everyone that is tried in the way of the spirit, nor even the half of them, and He knoweth the reason," and this has been taken to mean that in fact God, for reasons which He alone knows, does not *call* to this life all those who nevertheless aspire to it.

But this is to give to the words of the saint an interpretation which they do not fairly admit, for he says not that these persons are not *called* but that only a fraction of them are *raised* to contemplation— a very different thing. And he goes on to explain (*The Living Flame*, Str. 2, v. 5) that " God does not reserve such a lofty vocation for certain souls only: on the contrary, He is willing that all should embrace it. But He finds few who permit Him to work such sublime things in them. There are many who, when He sends them trials, shrink from the labour and refuse to bear with the dryness and mortification, instead of submitting, as they must, with perfect patience. Hence, finding them to be deficient in strength under the first graces which He bestows upon them for their purification, He stops, and their purification ceases, and He does no more to free them from the dust of earthly things that lies upon them, since this will demand of them greater courage and determination than they possess." The phrase " and He knows the reason " should be understood, therefore, to mean just that He knows—what neither we, nor perhaps they themselves, are aware of— that in the case of many (of the greater part, it should seem) the call will not meet with that generosity of response which is necessary if they are to come to its full consummation. This is quite in harmony with Our Lord's own words that " many are called but few are chosen "—not from any arbitrary discrimination, as it were, on the part of God, but because only a small proportion of the many who are called (that is, of the whole) are of such quality as will face the immense trials that are involved.

There are, in the works of St. John of the Cross, many passages confirmatory of this doctrine, so that the thesis remains intact that the grace of contemplation may, in fact, be desired and hoped for by all who have, by the Sacrament of Baptism, been raised to a participation in the Divine Life. Hence, it follows that it is an error to look upon the works of the great Doctor of Mysticism as pertinent only to the case of a handful of Christians, and as useless, if even not harmful, to the generality. Even those who will never go far along that Way must derive benefit (more, perhaps, than they would be willing to admit) from contact with ideas so lofty and so ennobling. And who knows what unsuspected force and heroism may not be stirred into activity by it ? At least, it will provide an ideal : and no one who is not grossly insensitive to what is fine and

noble, however remote-seeming, can fail to be the
better (even should that "better" be no more than
"humbler") for the glimpse of that wonderful
world which he will catch from the writings of the
saint. God *must* mean something different and be
something more to him in consequence : the supernatural *must* become more real to him : and just as
the study of a perfect work of art, however little we
be fitted fully to understand its excellence, will still
discontent us for ever afterwards with all that is
inferior, though we may not be able clearly to define
the grounds of our disagreement, so even this distant
Pisgah view of the Holy Land will make us forever
see the most common things of the spiritual life with
a brightness of vision that never could we otherwise
have imagined, though it should be our lot to finish
our days in the dim land of Moab.

To read and study the works of St. John of the
Cross should not, therefore, be looked upon as
something unusual or freakish, as it is often regarded :
nor, on the other hand, as denoting the possession
of special and extraordinary grace. As well might
an artist think it exceptional to study the works of
the great Masters of his craft, small though might be
his hope of ever emulating them. The trouble
really is that St. John is not "easy reading," so that
many are discouraged from the very outset and are
content to say that it is not for them. But the
reason of his apparent obscurity (for it is only
apparent, and yields to patience and humility) is
precisely that he is dealing with things which simply
will not go into words. But the mystic must speak :
he cannot be silent, as the sea cannot be still or fire
not burn. His trouble is that he can give us scarcely

more than an algebra of his secret, and to that we have not the complete key except at the price of being as he is himself. Certainly, if we approach such writings as these in the spirit of a scholar investigating a difficult intellectual problem, we shall never get beyond the threshold of their subject, because by so doing we should be dealing with it as if it were a matter capable of being exactly stated in terms of ordinary thought and experience; whereas it transcends both of these. It deals with principles and propositions which for the most part are intued rather than intellectually attained, and the language in which they are formulated (there being no other available) must inevitably, because of that, be largely metaphorical or analogical, and therefore very liable to misunderstanding. For this reason St. John of the Cross occupies the greater part of his writings in repeating in varying terms and from varying points of view a relatively small number of ideas. Indeed, one might almost say that he has but one idea, the absolute necessity, namely, of freeing our conceptions of God, and our method of approach to Him, from the hindrances occasioned by the discursive intellect, the imagination, and the sensitive will, this being preparatory to the acquisition of that " passivity " of soul which alone enables God to communicate Himself to us in the perfection which constitutes contemplation properly so called. The " Night " of which he speaks so terrifyingly—of the senses and of the spirit—are the processes by which this freedom is attained. They are both effect and cause of the establishment in the soul of that pure faith on which rests the whole of the mystic apprehension of God—two degrees of absolute trust in and committal to Him, based upon nothing of our own but upon Him alone. According to our natural mode of knowing, they seem to bring us nothing but extreme darkness and utter ignorance : but it is really this " natural " mode which causes actual darkness and ignorance, because it is inherently and incurably incapable of producing in the mind that light by which alone God is to be seen as He is. Not that in this world we can ever see Him as He is : but of the faith which is the substance of the mystical knowledge of God, St. John says that it is " luminous "—lighting the soul in which it is found in a way of which it can never, even to itself, give a satisfactory account : of which, indeed, if it tries to give an account, the result is only a deeper impression of obscurity. For there the speculative faculty gives no help : it is confined to the data afforded to it by the senses and by the experiences which come to it through them. But nothing of God can be directly apprehended by the senses.

Still less is the imagination of any use, and for a similar reason. The sensitive will, too, finds there no food for its appetite—again, because for such grounds of desire it is dependent upon the reason and the imagination. It is by no means that God is too " big " for these faculties to apprehend Him : the distinction is not of degree, but of kind : He is by His very nature inapprehensible by them, as colour is inapprehensible by touch or shape by hearing. The order of His Being has only this in common with ours (though indeed it is incorrect to speak of any community between us) that we are beings solely by participation in His absolute Being, yet not even so that we may speak of Him and of ourselves as in any sort of sense comparable. So the understanding must be silent, and the imagination closed, and the sensitive will quiescent, and only in this complete repose, this slumber, this night of the intellectual powers, is that superior part of the will (which without any natural self-regarding desire is to be turned upon the ultimate Object of all desire) free to seek out God Himself alone, for Himself alone. This, of course, means the utter surrender of every personal quest or ambition. The House must be at rest before the soul, inflamed with such an anxious love, is able to come forth unobserved into that darkness, that unknowing, which are the divine light and the supreme wisdom.

If one knew no more of the matter than this, one would easily gather how hard, how terrible, how almost unbearable is the way of the soul whom God leads through this illuminating obscurity—more and more into nothing, and nothing, and nothing. It calls for a breaking, one by one, of all ties and attachments, even the most intimate and excellent— " in order to have the All thou must leave the all! " —and with nothing, measurable by the old standards (which do not vanish so easily!), in exchange. Finally, happens the sublime paradox that one's happiness, beyond imagination perfect, is no other than the very happiness of God Himself, wholly and entirely His and wholly and entirely not ours; yet because we are created for no other end but that we should give the whole of our love to Him, at one and the same time most completely and supremely ours. Not " ours *and* His," but " ours *because* His."

No one has ever approached so nearly to an intelligible explanation of these mysteries as has St.

John of the Cross, because (among other reasons) no one has ever taken such enormous pains to analyse the details of this true Pilgrim's Progress or to state and re-state, now from one angle, now from another, with wealth of argument and sound philosophy and example and imagery, as he has done, the mighty simplicity of its principles. There remains, and must remain, a residue of what can be no further explained, and beyond this point the soul must go on alone. But its solitary way will be illumined by a steady development within it, in terms of its ever-growing experience (eluding even its own powers of statement) of the mystic life which the saint has laboured so hard to describe.

It is the peculiar merit and value of the present work that the author has assembled in logical order, in a chain of which each link is an advance in demonstration upon the preceding one, the very words which the saint himself used in elucidation of his own doctrine. Many an one, discouraged by the very richness and volume of St. John's exposition, will take new heart of grace as he reads this masterly digest of it. Hard sayings and paradoxes and seemingly dark problems will begin to yield up their secret to him. He will begin to realise that, after all, they do make sense! He will find with in-creasing pleasure that his own spiritual outlook and ideals are broadening and brightening and assuming a coherence and a purposiveness which clothe them with reality and attraction beyond words to estimate. And not only, as some might think, will this concern that lofty region in which alone the saint seems to move, but even in the humbler paths of the spiritual life (so unfortunately called " ordinary ") it will be found to discharge an important, perhaps an indispensable, function.

. . . . .

The English translation of the Works of St. John of the Cross used here is the well-known one by David Lewis. Recent scholarship has shown that this version is not always literally faithful to the text, but, since it unquestionably renders the meaning of the Saint with substantial accuracy, particularly in the passages used here, it is considered to be quite adequate for the practical purpose intended by this book.

SUMMARY OF CONTENTS [1]

PAGE

INTRODUCTION BY R. H. J. STEUART . . . v

THE ASCENT OF MOUNT CARMEL STANZAS
SUMMARISING THE DOCTRINE 1

PROLOGUE 3
NECESSITY OF SUFFERING—SOULS WHO MAKE NO
PROGRESS—UNWISE DIRECTORS—FOR WHOM THIS
BOOK IS INTENDED.

BOOK I.: THE DARK NIGHT OF SENSE AND
DESIRE 5
THE TWO NIGHTS—DARKNESS IS NECESSARY—PRO-
GRESSIVE DARKNESS—ABSENCE OF DESIRE—NECESSITY
OF MORTIFICATION—ALL DESIRES NOT EQUALLY
HARMFUL—VOLUNTARY DESIRES MUST DIE—HABITS OF
VOLUNTARY IMPERFECTION—§ ENTRY INTO THE NIGHT
OF THE SENSES—COUNSELS.

BOOK II.: THE ACTIVE NIGHT OF THE
SPIRIT 13
DIFFERENCES BETWEEN THE TWO NIGHTS—DARKNESS
AND EMPTINESS—UNION WITH GOD—DETACHMENT
AND FREEDOM—THE FOLLOWING OF CHRIST—REASON
NOT APT FOR UNION—§ SUPERNATURAL PERCEPTIONS—
§ NATURAL PERCEPTIONS AND MEDITATION—§ SIGNS
FOR LEAVING MEDITATION—LOVING ATTENTION—
THE HABIT OF CONTEMPLATION—§ OBSCURE AND
GENERAL KNOWLEDGE—RETURN TO MEDITATION—§
VISIONS—§ PURELY SPIRITUAL PERCEPTIONS—NO
ATTACHMENT TO VISIONS—§ REVELATIONS—KNOW-

[1] The chief sub-sections, here and in the text, are prefixed with the sign §

LEDGE OF PURE TRUTHS—DIVINE TOUCHES—INSIGHT—
§ INTERIOR LOCUTIONS—(1) SUCCESSIVE, (2) FORMAL,
(3) SUBSTANTIAL—§ SPIRITUAL IMPRESSIONS.

BOOK III.: PURGATION AND ACTIVE NIGHT OF THE MEMORY AND THE WILL . .   52

PART I.—THE MEMORY AND NATURAL APPREHENSIONS
—ANSWER TO A DOUBT—STRIPPING THE MEMORY—
UNION EMPTIES THE MEMORY—FOUR OBJECTIONS—
POWERLESSNESS OF THE DEVIL—EMPTINESS GIVES
PEACE—§ THE MEMORY AND SUPERNATURAL APPREHEN-
SIONS—HARM DONE BY ATTACHMENT TO THEM—
NATURAL ACTION OF THE SOUL—§ THE MEMORY AND
SPIRITUAL APPREHENSIONS.

PART II.—THE WILL   63

TEMPORAL GOODS—NATURAL GOODS—SENSIBLE
GOODS—MORAL GOODS—SUPERNATURAL GOODS—
SPIRITUAL GOODS—HOLY IMAGES—ORATORIES.

THE DARK NIGHT OF THE SOUL

BOOK I.: THE PASSIVE NIGHT OF SENSE .   71

NECESSITY OF THIS NIGHT—GENERAL IMPERFECTIONS
—SPIRITUAL IMPERFECTIONS: (1) PRIDE, (2) SPIRITUAL
AVARICE, (3) SENSUALITY, (4) ANGER, (5) SPIRITUAL
GLUTTONY, (6) ENVY AND SLOTH—§ WHAT THE DARK
NIGHT IS—RECOLLECTION IS FAVOURABLE—THREE
SIGNS OF THE NIGHT—CONDUCT: PASSIVITY—PASSAGE
TO CONTEMPLATION—NEED OF A GOOD DIRECTOR—
ABANDONMENT OF MEDITATION—FIRST IMPRESSIONS—
THE NARROW GATE—ADVANTAGES OF THIS NIGHT—
MOMENTS OF ILLUMINATION—THE DEVIL—DURATION
OF PURIFICATION.

BOOK II.: THE PASSIVE NIGHT OF THE SPIRIT 91

TRANSITION BETWEEN THE TWO NIGHTS—PHYSICAL EFFECTS—IMPERFECTIONS OF PROFICIENTS—CONTEMPLATION IN DARKNESS—EFFECTS OF THE NIGHT—BURNING IN DARKNESS—LOVE AND KNOWLEDGE—THE UNDERSTANDING MUST BE PURIFIED—DARKNESS AND SUFFERING—SUMMARY—THE DESIRES ARE CALMED—SECURITY OF THIS STATE—PROGRESS IN DARKNESS—THIS CONTEMPLATION IS SECRET—THE DEGREES OF THE MYSTICAL LADDER—ATTACKS OF THE DEVIL—SUBSTANTIAL TOUCHES—THE HIGHEST DEGREE OF PRAYER.

THE LIVING FLAME OF LOVE

STANZAS 116

PROLOGUE 117

THE SOUL TRANSFORMED—THE PURGATIVE WAY—PERSEVERANCE—THE BURNING TOUCH OF LOVE—SUBSTANTIAL TOUCHES—THEIR ABUNDANT GAIN—WHY FEW ATTAIN TO ESPOUSALS—DEATH TO HUMAN ACTIVITY.

THE CONDUCT OF CONTEMPLATIVE SOULS 124

THE DIRECTOR AND MEDITATION—PASSAGE TO CONTEMPLATION—THE SOUL IS PASSIVE—IGNORANT DIRECTORS—OBJECTIONS TO PASSIVITY—LOVE AND KNOWLEDGE—RESPONSIBILITY OF DIRECTORS—THE DEVIL—THE SENSE OF THE SOUL—THE AWAKENING OF THE BRIDGEGROOM.

THE SPIRITUAL CANTICLE

THE SONG OF THE SOUL 141

PAGE

I. THE PURGATIVE WAY 149

TORMENT OF ABSENCE—GOD IS HIDDEN—HOW TO SEEK
GOD—LANGUOR OF LOVE—THE SOUL'S SUFFERINGS
AND ACTIVITIES—DESIRE FOR GOD—AGONY OF THE
SOUL—WOUNDED BY LOVE.

II. THE ILLUMINATIVE WAY . . . 156

§ THE SPIRITUAL BETROTHAL—KNOWLEDGE IS STILL
DARK—DAWN—NOT YET PERFECT PEACE—TROUBLES
CAUSED BY THE DEVIL—DESIRE FOR DETACHMENT—
SUFFERING FROM CLEARER KNOWLEDGE—LONGING FOR
CONTACT—STRENGTH OF THE SOUL—PEACE AND
PLENITUDE.

III. THE UNITIVE WAY 167

§ THE SPIRITUAL MARRIAGE—THE BRIDEGROOM
REVEALS HIS SECRETS—LOVE DOES NOT DEPEND ON
KNOWLEDGE—THE SOUL INEBRIATED WITH LOVE—
CENTRED IN LOVE—§ THE CONTEMPLATIVE LIFE—
ACTIVITY VAIN WITHOUT CONTEMPLATION—ALONE
GOD—NECESSITY OF SUFFERING.

THE ASCENT OF MOUNT CARMEL

ARGUMENT[1]

THE following stanzas are a summary of the doctrine contained in this book of the Ascent of Mount Carmel. They also describe how we are to ascend to the summit of it, that is, to the high state of perfection, called here union of the soul with God. I place all the stanzas together, because that which I have to say is founded upon them. . . .

The first two stanzas explain the two spiritual purgations of the sensual and spiritual part of man, and the other six the various and admirable effects of the spiritual enlightenment and union of love with God.

> In a dark night,
> With anxious love inflamed,
> O happy lot!
> Forth unobserved I went,
> My house being now at rest.
>
> In darkness and in safety,
> By the secret ladder, disguised,
> O happy lot!
> In darkness and concealment,
> My house being now at rest.

[1] These verses form the argument of both the *Ascent* and the *Dark Night*. The second paragraph given above is taken from the *Dark Night*. Actually the *Dark Night* is incomplete, six stanzas out of eight remain without explanation. The *Living Flame* may, up to a point, fill this gap.

In that happy night
In secret, seen of none,
Seeing nought myself,
Without other light or guide
Save that which in my heart was burning.

That light guided me
More surely than the noonday sun
To the place where He was waiting for me,
Whom I knew well,
And where none appeared.

O guiding night ;
O night more lovely than the dawn ;
O night that hast united
The lover with His beloved,
And changed her into her love

On my flowery bosom,
Kept whole for Him alone,
There He reposed and slept ;
And I caressed Him, and the waving
Of the cedars fanned Him.

As I scattered His hair in the breeze
That blew from the turret,
He struck me on the neck
With His gentle hand,
And all sensation left me.

I continued in oblivion lost,
My head was resting on my love ;
Lost to all things and myself,
And, amid the lilies forgotten,
Threw all my cares away.

THE ASCENT OF MOUNT CARMEL

PROLOGUE

THE NECESSITY OF SUFFERING

So great are the trials, and so profound the darkness, spiritual as well as corporal, through which souls must pass, if they will attain to perfection, that no human learning can explain them, nor experience describe them. He only who has passed through them can know them, but even he cannot explain them.

SOULS WHO MAKE NO PROGRESS

Many persons begin to walk in the way of virtue—our Lord longing to lead them into the dark night that they may travel onwards into the divine union—but make no progress; sometimes because they will not enter upon this night, nor suffer Him to lead them into it; and sometimes also because they do not understand their own state, and are destitute of fit and wise directors who may guide them to the summit of the mount.

How miserable it is to see many souls, to whom God has given grace to advance—and who, had they taken courage, would have reached perfection—remain ungenerous in their dealing with God, through want of will or through ignorance, or because they have no one to direct their steps, and to teach them how to go onwards from the beginning. And in the end, when our Lord has compassion on them, and leads them on in spite of these hindrances, they arrive late, with much difficulty, and less **merit**, because they have not submitted themselves to His ways, nor suffered Him to plant their feet on the pure and certain road of union. Though it is true that God, Who leads them, can do so without these helps, still, because they do not yield themselves up to Him, they make less progress on the road, resisting their guide ; and they merit less because they do not submit their will, whereby their sufferings are increased.

There are souls who, instead of abandoning themselves to the care and protection of God, hinder Him rather by their indiscreet behaviour, or resistance. . . . .

UNWISE DIRECTORS

Some confessors and spiritual directors, because they have no perception or experience of these ways, are a hindrance and an evil, rather than a help to such souls. . . . When God leads anyone along the highest road of obscure contemplation and dryness, such an one will think himself lost ; and in this darkness and trouble, distress and temptation, some will be sure to tell him, like the comforters of Job, that his sufferings are the effects of melancholy, or of disordered health, or of natural temperament, or, it may be, of some secret sin for which God has abandoned him. Thus they multiply the sorrows of this poor soul, for his greatest trial is the knowledge of his own misery.

They do not understand that this is not the time for such acts as frequent general confessions ; it is now the day of God's purgation, when they ought to leave him alone, comforting him, indeed, and encouraging him to bear his trials patiently until God shall be pleased to deliver him ; for until then, notwithstanding all they may say or do, there can be no relief.

FOR WHOM THIS BOOK IS INTENDED

I am treating here of a solid and substantial doctrine suited to all, if they seek to advance to that detachment of spirit which is here described. My principal object, however, is not to address myself to all, but only to certain persons of our holy order of Mount Carmel. . . .

BOOK I

THE DARK NIGHT OF SENSE AND DESIRE

THE TWO NIGHTS

IN order to reach perfection, the soul has to pass, ordinarily, through two kinds of night, which spiritual writers call purgations, or purifications, of the soul, and which I have called night, because in the one as well as in the other the soul travels, as it were, by night, in darkness.

The first night is the night, or purgation, of the sensual part of the soul, which is the privation of all desire, wrought by God. . . . The second night is the night of the spiritual part, which is for those who are more advanced, when God wishes to bring them into union with Himself.

DARKNESS IS NECESSARY

The soul cannot enter into the night of itself, because no one is able of his own strength to empty his heart of all desires, so as to draw near unto God.

PROGRESSIVE DARKNESS

The night is divided into three parts. The first . . . may be likened to the commencement of night when material objects begin to be invisible. The second . . . may be compared to midnight, which is utter darkness. The third resembles the close of night, which is God, when the dawn of day is at hand.

ABSENCE OF DESIRE

There is no detachment, if desire remains . . . detachment . . . consists in suppressing desire, and avoiding pleasure; it is this that sets the soul free, even though possession may be still retained. It is not the things of this world that occupy or injure the soul, for they do not enter within, but rather the wish for, and desire of them, which abide within it.

THE NECESSITY OF MORTIFICATION

The affection and attachment which the soul feels for the creature renders the soul its equal and its like, and the greater the affection the greater will be the likeness. Love begets a likeness between the lover and the object of his love.

God did not give the manna to the people of Israel till the corn they had brought from Egypt had failed them, thereby showing us that everything must be given up, for the bread of angels is not given to, neither is it meant for, that palate which is pleased with the bread of man. He who feeds on strange meats, and is delighted therewith, not only disqualifies himself for the reception of the Holy Ghost, but also provokes God to anger exceedingly, as all do who, while they seek spiritual food, are not content with God only, but intermingle therewith carnal and earthly satisfactions.

Oh, would that spiritual persons knew how they are losing the good things of the Spirit, abundantly furnished, because they will not raise up their desires above trifles, and how they might have the sweetness of all things in the pure food of the Spirit if they would only forgo them. But as they will not, so they shall not have such sweetness The people of Israel perceived not the sweetness of every taste in the manna, though it was there, because they would not limit their desires to it alone.   The sweetness and strength of the manna was not for them, not because it was not there, but because they longed for other meats beside it.

Under the old law, the altar of sacrifice was to be hollow within.   " Thou shalt not make it solid, but empty and hollow in the inside."[1]   It is the will of God that the soul should be empty of all created things, so that it may become a fitting altar of His Majesty.

Even one unruly desire, though not a mortal sin, sullies and deforms the soul, and indisposes it for the perfect union with God, until it be cast away.

ALL DESIRES ARE NOT EQUALLY HARMFUL

All desires are not equally hurtful, neither do they all perplex the soul in the same degree. I am speaking of those which are voluntary: for the natural desires, when we do not consent to them, and when they do not pass beyond the first move-ments, do but slightly or not at all stand in the way of union. By natural and first movements I mean all those in which the rational will had no share,

[1] Exod. xxvii. 8.

either before or after they arose : for to banish and mortify these completely is, in this life, impossible. The hindrance which these create is not such as to prevent the divine union, though they may not be wholly mortified ; they may remain in their natural state, and yet the soul in its spiritual part may be most free from them. For it will sometimes happen that the soul enjoys the profound union of quiet in the will, while these remain in the sensual portion of man's nature, but having no communication with the spiritual portion occupied in prayer.

VOLUNTARY DESIRES MUST DIE

All the other voluntary desires, whether of mortal sins, which are the most grievous, or of venial sins, which are less so, or imperfections only, which are still less so, must be banished away, and the soul which would attain to perfect union must be delivered from them all, however slight they may be. The reason is this : the state of divine union consists in the total transformation of the will into the will of God, in such a way that every movement of the will shall be always the movement of the will of God only. . . . If the soul knowingly cleaves to any imperfection, contrary to the will of God, His will is not done, for the soul wills that which God wills not. . . . I say knowingly, for without deliberation and a clear perception of what we are doing, or because it is not wholly in our power, we may easily give way to imperfections and venial sins. . . . It is of such sins as these, not so entirely voluntary, that it is written : " A just man shall fall seven times, and shall rise again."[1]

[1] Prov. xxiv. 16.

HABITS OF VOLUNTARY IMPERFECTIONS

Some habits of voluntary imperfections, so far as they are never perfectly overcome, hinder not only the divine union, but our progress towards perfection.

These habitual imperfections are, for instance, much talking, certain attachments, which we never resolve to break through—such as to individuals, to a book or a cell, to a particular food, to certain society, the satisfaction of one's taste, science, news, and such things.

§ ENTRY INTO THE NIGHT OF THE SENSES

Ordinarily, the soul enters this night in two ways; one is the active way, the other is the passive. The active way is that by which the soul is able to make, and does make, efforts of its own to enter in, assisted by divine grace. Of this I shall speak in the instructions that follow. The passive way is that in which the soul does nothing as of itself, neither does it make therein any efforts of its own; but it is God who works in it, giving special aids, and the soul is, as it were, patient, freely consenting thereto.[1]

COUNSELS FOR ENTERING
THE NIGHT OF THE SENSES

1. Be continually careful and earnest in imitating Christ in everything, conforming thyself to

[1] The passive night is described in the book of the *Dark Night*.

His life : for this end thou must meditate thereon, that thou mayest know how to imitate it, and conduct thyself in all things as He would have done Himself.

2. To do this well, every satisfaction offered to the senses, which is not for God's honour and glory, must be renounced and rejected for the love of Jesus Christ. . . . For instance, if the pleasure of listening to anything which tends not to the service of God presents itself, seek not that pleasure, neither give ear to what is said. . . . Practise the same mortification with respect to the other senses, as far as possible ; and if it be not possible, it will be enough not to seek the pleasure that is offered. . . . The practice of this counsel will bring with it great profit in a short time.

In order to mortify and calm the four natural passions of joy, hope fear and grief . . . the following instructions are a perfect means of great merit and the source of great virtues :—

Strive always, not after that which is most easy, but after that which is most difficult.

Not after that which is most pleasant, but after that which is most unpleasant.

Not after that which giveth pleasure, but after that which giveth none.

Not after that which is consoling, but after that which is afflictive.

Not after that which ministers repose, but after that which ministers labour.

Not after great things, but after little things.

Not after that which is higher and precious, but after that which is lower and despised.

Strive not to desire anything, but rather nothing.

Do those things which bring thee into contempt, and desire that others also may do them.

Speak disparagingly of thyself, and contrive that others may do so too.

Think humbly and contemptuously of thyself, and desire that others may do so also.

BOOK II

THE ACTIVE NIGHT OF THE SPIRIT

THERE is no means of union with God except faith. After traversing the night of sense, the soul should perfect its faith by the first mortification of the spirit, that of the understanding.

DIFFERENCES BETWEEN THE TWO NIGHTS

The anxieties of sensible love were necessary . . . to journey in the night of sense, and to be detached from all objects of the same. But in order to perfect the tranquillity of the house of the spirit, no more is required than the concentration of all the powers of the soul, all its pleasures and spiritual desires, in pure faith.

In the night of sense, there remains still some light, because the understanding remains, and the reason also, which are not blind. But in this spiritual night, the night of faith, all is darkness, both in the understanding and the sense.

The soul, when it least uses its own proper ability, travels most securely, because it walks most by faith.

THE SOUL MUST BE IN DARKNESS AND EMPTINESS

The soul, to be rightly guided by faith towards union, must be in darkness, not only as to that part thereof—the sensual and the inferior, of which I have already spoken—which regards temporal and created things, but also as to that part thereof, the rational and the superior, of which I am now speaking, which regards God and spiritual things.

Inasmuch as this union and transformation are not cognisable by sense or any human power, the soul must be completely and voluntarily empty of all that can enter into it, of every affection and inclination, so far as it concerns itself. Who shall hinder God from doing His own will in a soul that is resigned, detached, and self-annihilated? The soul must be emptied of all that its own powers are capable of; and however great may be its supernatural endowments, it must be as it were detached from them, in darkness like a blind man, leaning on the obscure faith, and taking it for its light and guide; not trusting to anything it understands, tastes, feels, or imagines—for all this is darkness, which will lead it astray, or keep it back; and faith is above all understanding, taste, and sense.

If the soul be not blind herein, and in total darkness as to all such things, it will never reach to those higher things which faith teaches. A blind man, if he be not totally blind, will not commit himself wholly to his guide, but because he sees a little he thinks a certain road secure, not seeing another which is better.

The soul, if it leans upon any understanding, sense, or feeling of its own—all this, whatever it may be, is very little and very unlike to God—in order to travel along this road, is most easily led astray or hindered. . . . He that will attain to the union of God must not rely on his own understanding, nor lean upon his own imagination, sense, or feeling, but must believe in the perfection of the divine essence, which is not cognisable by the understanding, desire, imagination, nor any sense of man.

To be perfectly united in this life to God in grace and love, the soul must live in utter darkness as to all that can enter by the eye, all that the ear receives, all that the fancy may imagine, or the heart conceive, which here signifies the soul. Greatly embarrassed, then, is the soul, on the road of the divine union, when it leans at all on its own understanding, sense, imagination, judgment, will or any habits of its own, or anything peculiar to itself, not knowing how to free and detach itself therefrom. For, as I have said, the goal to which it tends is beyond this, though this may be the highest thing it may know or feel, and it must, therefore go beyond, passing on to that which it knows not.[1]

[1] " But above all, if we desire to taste God, or to experience Life Eternal in our own selves, we must, passing beyond reason, first enter into God by Faith ; there we must remain simple, despoiled and free of all images, and lifted by love to an open nakedness in our higher memory. For when we pass beyond all things through love, and, dying to all considerations, we go on to a state of ignorance and darkness, we there suffer the action and higher information of the Eternal Word, the image of the Father. Our spirit being free from activity, we receive the incomprehensible brightness which enwraps us and penetrates us, as the air is bathed in the light of the sun. And this brightness is nothing else than limitless contemplation and beholding. What we are that we penetrate in beholding, and what we thus penetrate that we are ; for our spirit, our life, our being, are all elevated in a manner both one and simple to the Truth which is God. In this simple beholding we are one life and one spirit with God : This is what I call a contemplative life."—RUYSBROECK : *The Ring*, Chapter IX.

On this road, therefore, to abandon one's own way is to enter on the true way, or, to speak more correctly, to pass onwards to the goal; and to forsake one's own way is to enter on that which has none, namely God. For the soul that attains to this state has no ways or methods of its own, neither does it, nor can it, lean upon anything of the kind. I mean ways of understanding, perceiving, or feeling, though it has all ways at the same time, as one who, possessing nothing, yet possesseth everything. For the soul courageously resolved on passing, interiorly and exteriorly beyond the limits of its own nature, enters illimitably within the supernatural, which has no measure, but contains all measure eminently within itself. To arrive there is to depart hence, going away, out of oneself, as far as possible, from this vile state to that which is the highest of all. Therefore, rising above all that may be known and understood, temporally and spiritually, the soul must earnestly desire to reach that which in this life cannot be known, and which the heart cannot conceive; and, leaving behind all actual and possible taste and feeling of sense and spirit, must desire earnestly to arrive at that which transcends all sense and all feeling.

In order that the soul may be free and unembarrassed for this end, it must in no wise attach itself . . . to anything it may receive in the sense or spirit, but esteem such as of much less importance. For the more importance the soul attributes to what it understands, feels, and imagines, and the greater the estimation it holds it in, whether it be spiritual or not, the more it detracts from the supreme good, and the greater will be its delay in attaining to it. On the other hand, the less it esteems all that it may have in comparison with the supreme good, the more does it magnify and esteem the supreme good, and consequently the greater the progress towards it.

THE NATURE OF UNION WITH GOD

In every soul, even that of the greatest sinner in the world, God dwells, and is substantially present. This way of union or presence of God, in the order of nature, subsists between Him and all His creatures. By this He preserves them in being, and if He withdraws it they immediately perish and cease to be.

And so when I speak of the union of the soul with God, I do not mean this substantial presence which is in every creature, but that union and transformation of the soul in God by love, which is only then accomplished when there subsists the likeness which love begets. For this reason shall this union be called the union of likeness, as the other is essential or substantial union; this latter one is natural, the other is supernatural, which takes effect when two wills, the will of God and the will of the soul, are conformed together, neither desiring aught repugnant to the other.

That soul has greater communion with God which is most advanced in love, that is, whose will is most conformable to the will of God. And that soul which has reached perfect conformity and resemblance is perfectly united with, and supernaturally transformed in, God.

For which cause, therefore, as I have already explained, the more the soul cleaves to created things, relying on its own strength, by habit and inclination, the less is it disposed for this union, because it does not completely resign itself into the hands of God, that He may transform it supernaturally. The soul has need, therefore, to be detached from . . . its own understanding, liking, and feeling and all that is unlike to, and not in conformity with, God, so that He, Who communicates Himself to it naturally, in the order of nature, may also communicate Himself supernaturally, in the order of grace.

The soul, by resigning itself to the divine light, that is, by removing from itself every spot and stain of the creature, which is to keep the will perfectly united to the will of God—for to love Him is to labour to detach ourselves from, and to divest ourselves of, everything which is not God, for God's sake—becomes immediately enlightened by, and transformed in, God; because He communicates His own supernatural being in such a way that the soul seems to be God Himself and to possess the things of God. Such a union is then wrought when God bestows on the soul[1] that supreme grace which makes the things of God and the soul one by the transformation which renders the one a partaker of the other. The soul seems to be God rather than itself, and indeed is God by participation, though in reality preserving its own natural substance as distinct from God as it did before, although transformed in Him, as the window preserves its own substance distinct from that of the rays of the sun shining through it and making it light.

Hence it becomes more evident that the fitting disposition for this union is, not that the soul should understand, taste, feel, or imagine anything on the subject of the nature of God, or any other thing whatever, but only that pureness and love which is perfect resignation, and complete detachment from all things for God alone.

But that soul which does not attain to that degree of purity corresponding with the light and vocation it has received from God, will never obtain true peace and contentment, because it has not attained to that detachment and emptiness of its powers which are requisite for pure union.

Keep in mind, however, that I am now speaking specially of those who have begun to enter the state of contemplation. For, as to beginners, this must be discussed at greater length, which I shall do when I shall have to treat of what is peculiar to them.

DETACHMENT AND FREEDOM ARE NECESSARY

" Few there are that find the narrow gate." Mark here the reason of this saying, which is that there are but few who understand how, and desire, to enter into this supreme detachment and emptiness of spirit.

To follow Christ is to deny self ; this is not that other course which is nothing but to seek oneself in God, which is the very opposite of love. For to seek self in God is to seek for comfort and refreshment from God. But to seek God in Himself is not only to be willingly deprived of this thing and of that for God, but to incline ourselves to will and choose for Christ's sake whatever is most disagreeable, whether proceeding from God or from the world ; this is to love God.

The way of God consisteth not in the multiplicity of meditations, ways of devotion or sweetness, though these may be necessary for beginners, but in one necessary thing only, in knowing how to deny ourselves in earnest, inwardly and outwardly, giving ourselves up to suffer for Christ's sake, and annihilating ourselves utterly. He who shall exercise himself herein, will then find all this and much more. And if he be deficient at all in this exercise, which is the sum and root of all virtue, all he may do will be but beating the air; utterly profitless, notwithstanding great meditations and communications.

THE FOLLOWING OF CHRIST

Christ cried out on the cross, " My God, my God, why hast thou forsaken Me ? " This was the greatest sensible abandonment of His whole life ; and it was then that He wrought the greatest work of His whole life of miracles and of wonders, the reconciliation and union with God by grace of all mankind. This He accomplished at that very moment when He was most annihilated in all things, brought lowest in the estimation of men, for when they saw Him dying on the ignominious tree, they showed Him no reverence, nay, rather they stood by and derided Him. Then, too, was He brought lowest in His very nature, for that was as it were annihilated when He died. . . .

But let me now address myself to the understanding of the spiritual man, and in an especial manner to him whom God in His goodness has raised up to the state of contemplation. . . .

REASON IS NOT CAPABLE OF GIVING THAT KNOW-
LEDGE OF GOD WHICH ACHIEVES UNION WITH HIM

Nothing that the imagination may conceive or
the understanding comprehend, in this life, is or can
be a proximate means of union with God. For if
we speak of natural knowledge; the understanding
is incapable of comprehending anything unless it be
presented to it under forms and images by the bodily
senses. . . . Again, if we speak of supernatural
acts—as far as possible in this life—the understanding in its bodily prison has neither the disposition nor the capacity requisite for the reception of
the clear knowledge of God.

Elias, our father, covered his face on the mountain,
in the presence of God.[1] By that action he taught
us that he made his understanding blind, not ventur-
ing to apply an instrument so vile to a matter so
high; and that he perceived clearly, that however
much he saw or understood, all would be most
unlike unto God, and far distant from Him.

No knowledge, therefore, and no conceptions in
this mortal life can serve as proximate means of this
high union of the love of God. All that the understanding may comprehend; all that the will may be
satisfied with; and all that the imagination may
conceive, is most unlike unto God, and most
disproportionate to Him.

Hence it is that contemplation, by which God
enlightens the understanding, is called mystical

[1] III Kings xix. 13.

theology, that is, the secret wisdom of God, because it is a secret even to the understanding which receives it. St. Dionysius calls it a ray of darkness. . . . It is therefore clear that the understanding must be blind, as to every path along which it has to travel, in order to be united with God.

§ SUPERNATURAL PERCEPTIONS RECEIVED THROUGH THE SENSES ARE TO BE REJECTED

Spiritual men are occasionally liable to representations and objects set before them in a supernatural way. They sometimes see the forms and figures of those of another life, saints, or angels, good and evil, or certain extraordinary lights and brightness. They hear strange words, sometimes seeing those who utter them, and sometimes not. They have a sensible perception at times of most sweet odours, without knowing whence they proceed. Their sense of taste is also deliciously affected ; and that of the touch so sweetly caressed at times that the bones and the marrow exalt and rejoice, bathed, as it were, in joy. This delight is like to that which we call the unction of the Spirit, flowing from Him through all the senses of simple souls. And this sensible sweetness is wont to affect spiritual persons, because of that sensible devotion, more or less, which they have, every one in his own measure.

Still, though all these may happen to the bodily senses in the way of God, we must never rely on them, nor encourage them ; nay, rather we must fly from them, without examining whether they be good or evil. For, inasmuch as they are exterior and in the body, there is the less certainty of their being from God. It is more natural that God should communicate Himself through the spirit—wherein there is greater security and profit for the soul— than through the senses, wherein there is usually much danger and delusion, because the bodily sense decides upon, and judges, spiritual things, thinking them to be what itself feels them to be.

The devil has more influence in that which is exterior and corporeal, and can more easily deceive us therein than in what is more interior. And these bodily forms and objects, the more exterior they are, the less do they profit the interior spiritual man. . . .

Even if these things communicate some spirituality, as is always the case when they proceed from God, yet it is much less than it would have been had they been more spiritual and interior; and thus they become more easily and readily occasions of error, presumption, and vanity. As they are so palpable and so material they excite the senses greatly, and the soul is led to consider them the more important, the more they are felt. It runs after them and abandons the secure guidance of faith, thinking that the light they give is a guide and means to that which it desires, union with God. Thus the soul, the more it makes of such things, the more it strays from the perfect way and means, that is, the faith.

We must always reject and disregard these representations and sensations. For even if some of them were from God, no wrong is offered to Him, because the effect and fruit, which He desires to bring forth in the soul, is not the less accomplished when that soul rejects them and seeks them not.

§ NATURAL PERCEPTIONS OF THE IMAGINATION ; MEDITATION

The two powers of imagination and fancy serve for meditation, which is a discursive act by means of imagery, forms, and figures, wrought and fashioned in the senses. We picture to ourselves Christ on the cross, or bound to the pillar, or God sitting on His throne in great majesty. So also we imagine glory as a most beautiful light, and represent before ourselves any other object, human or divine, of which the faculty of imagination is capable.

All these imaginations and apprehensions are to be emptied out of the soul, which must remain in darkness so far as it concerns the senses, in order that we may attain to the divine union, because they bear no proportion to the proximate means of union with God ; as neither do bodily things, the objects of the five exterior senses.

Though such considerations, forms, and methods of meditation may be necessary for beginners, in order to inflame and fill their souls with love, through the instrumentality of sense, as I shall explain hereafter—and though they may serve as remote means of union, through which souls must usually pass to the goal and resting-place of spiritual repose—still they must so make use of them as to pass beyond them, and not dwell upon them forever. If we dwell upon them we shall never reach the goal, which is not like the remote means, neither has it any proximate relation with them.

Great, therefore, is the mistake of those spiritual persons who, having laboured to draw near unto God by means of imagery, forms, and meditations, such as become beginners—while God would attract them to the more spiritual, interior, and unseen good, by depriving them of the joy and sweetness of discursive meditation—do not accept the guidance, neither venture nor know how to detach themselves from these sensible methods to which they have been accustomed. They retain these methods still, seeking to advance by them and by meditation upon exterior forms, as before, thinking that it must be so always.

They take great pains in the matter, but find very little sweetness or none; nay rather, dryness, weariness, and disquiet of soul increase and grow the more they search after the sweetness they had before, because it is now impossible for them to have it as they had it as first. The soul has no more pleasure in the food . . . which was of the senses, but requires another of greater delicacy, interior, and less cognisable by the senses, consisting, not in the travail of the imagination, but in the repose of the soul, and in that quietness thereof, which is more spiritual. The more the soul advances in spirituality the more it ceases from the operations of its faculties on particular objects; for it then gives itself up to one sole, pure, and general act; and so its powers cease from the practice of that method by which they once travelled towards the point to which the soul was tending.

How sad it is to see men who, when the soul would be at peace in the repose of interior quiet, where God fills it with refreshment and peace, disturb it, draw it away to outward things, compel it to travel again along the road it had passed, and to abandon the goal where it reposes, for the sake of the means and considerations which guided it to its rest. This is not effected without loathing and repugnance on the part of the soul, which would repose in this tranquillity as in its proper place—as it happens to him who after toilsome labour has attained repose; for when he is made to return to his work he feels it painfully. And as they do not understand the secret of their new condition, they imagine themselves to be idle, doing nothing; and so do not suffer themselves to be at rest, but strive to reproduce their former reflections and discursive acts.[1] They are therefore full of dryness and

[1] Saint Chantal "had a quick and fertile imagination and the lower parts of her soul made great resistance to condescending to this peaceable repose and most holy inactivity, always wishing to do and to act, however truly her attraction and her way lay towards being totally passive."—CHAUGY: *Vie de St. Chantal.*

"My very dear child, we must quiet our activity of mind."—ST. FRANÇOIS DE SALES TO ST. CHANTAL.

"I saw that I do not limit my mind enough simply to prayer, that I always want to do something myself in it, wherein I do very wrong. . . . I wish most definitely to cut off and separate my mind, from all that, and to hold it, with all my strength as much as I can, in this sole regard and simple unity."—ST. CHANTAL: *Oeuvres Complétes*, Vol. II.

"I again beg my most dear Lord the aid of Holy Obedience to stop this wretched runaway,"—*Ibid.*

". . . by allowing the fear of being ineffectual enter into this state of prayer, and wishing to accomplish something myself, I spoilt it all. And I am still often attacked by this same fear. The activity of my mind is so great that I always feel a great need to support and encouragement with regard to it. Alas, my beloved Father so often told me so."—*Ibid. Lettres*, Vol. IV.

trouble, because they seek there for sweetness where there is no longer sweetness for them.

To these my counsel is—learn to abide with attention in loving waiting upon God in the state of quiet; give no heed to your imagination, nor to its operations, for now, as I have said, the powers of the soul are at rest, and are not exercised, except in the sweet and pure waiting of love. If at times they are excited, it is not violently, nor with meditation elaborately prepared, but by the sweetness of love, more under the influence of God than of the ability of the soul.

§ SIGNS FOR LEAVING MEDITATION

It is necessary to explain when the spiritual man should abstain from the meditation which rests on imaginary forms and mental representations, in order that he may abstain from it neither sooner nor later than when the Spirit calls him. For as it is necessary to abstain from it at the proper time, in order to draw near unto God, that we may not be hindered by it, so also must we not cease from it before the time, lest we go backwards: for though all that the powers of the soul may apprehend cannot be proximate means of union for those who have made some spiritual progress, still they serve, as remote means, to dispose and habituate the minds of beginners to that which is spiritual by means of the senses.

First Sign: When he finds he cannot meditate nor exert his imagination, nor derive any satisfaction from it, as he was wont to do—when he finds dryness there, where he was accustomed to fix the senses and draw forth sweetness—then the time is come. But while he finds sweetness, and is able to meditate as usual, let him not cease therefrom, except when his soul is in peace, of whom I shall speak when describing the third sign.

Second Sign : When he sees that he has no inclination to fix the imagination or the senses on particular objects, exterior or interior. I do not mean when the imagination neither comes nor goes —for it is disorderly even in the most complete self-recollection—but only when the soul derives no pleasure from tying it down deliberately to other matters.

Third Sign : The third sign is the most certain of the three, namely, when the soul delights to be alone, waiting lovingly on God, without any particular considerations, in interior peace, quiet, and repose, when the acts and exercises of the understanding, memory, and will, at least discursively—which is the going from one subject to another—have ceased ; nothing remaining except that knowledge and attention, general and loving, of which I have spoken, without the particular perception of aught else. [1]

[1] " There are three signs which make us know when we must reasonably reject these images so that we should not pursue them unnecessarily—or waste our time pursuing them—and that we should retain no more than is necessary.

" 1. When we have a distaste for all conceptions and for all that we hear said.

" 2. When nothing that enters our thoughts, that strikes our ears, causes us any pleasure.

" 3. When we feel in ourselves a thirst and a burning desire for the Sovereign Good to which we know not how to attain—so that we say in the ardour which drives us more and more ' My Lord and my God, I can go no further. It is for me to pray to you and for you to grant my prayer.'

" When a soul feels thus driven, she not only may with reason, but she even must deny to herself all those images, however holy, of which we have spoken."—TAULER: *Institutions*, Chapter XXXV.

The spiritual man must have observed these three signs together, at least, before he can venture with safety to abandon the state of meditation for that of the way of spiritual contemplation. It is not enough for him to observe the first without the second, for it may happen that he cannot meditate on the things of God, as before, because of distractions and the absence of due preparation. He must therefore have regard to the second sign, and see whether he has no inclination or desire to think of other things. For when this inability to fix the imagination and the senses on the things of God proceeds from distraction or lukewarmness, the soul readily inclines to other matters, and these lead it away from God.

Neither is it sufficient to have observed the first and second sign if we do not also discern the third. For though we cannot meditate or think on the things of God, and have no pleasure either in dwelling upon anything else ; yet this may be the effect of melancholy or some other oppression of the brain or the heart, which is wont to produce a certain suspension of our faculties, so that we think upon nothing, nor desire to do so, nor have any inclination thereto, but rather remain in a kind of soothing astonishment. By way of defence against this, we must be sure of the third sign, which is a loving knowledge and attention in peace, as I have said.

THE LOVING ATTENTION NOT AT FIRST PERCEIVED

In the commencement of the state this loving knowledge is, as it were, imperceptible, because it is then wont to be, in the first place, most subtle and delicate, and, as it were, unfelt ; and because, in the second place, the soul, having been accustomed to meditation, which is more cognisable by sense, does not perceive, and, as it were, does not feel this new condition, not subject to sense, and which is purely spiritual.

This is the case especially when, through not understanding his condition, the spiritual man will not allow himself to rest therein, but will strive after that which is cognisable by sense. This striving, notwithstanding the abundance of loving interior peace, robs him of the sense and enjoyment of it. But the more the soul is disposed for this tranquillity, the more will it grow therein continually ; and the more conscious it will be of this general loving knowledge of God, which is sweeter to it than all besides, because it brings with it peace and rest, sweetness and delight without trouble.

THE FITNESS OF THE SIGNS
THE SOUL ATTAINS TO THE HABIT OF
CONTEMPLATION

The end of meditation and reflection on the things of God is to have the knowledge and the love of Him as its fruit. Each time this is done, it is an act, and as acts often repeated produce habits, so, many acts of loving knowledge continuously made by the soul, beget the habit thereof in the course of time. God is wont at times to effect this without these acts of meditation—at least without many of them—leading souls at once into the state of contemplation. Thus, what the soul obtained before, at intervals, by dint of meditation, in particular acts of knowledge, is now by practice converted into the habit and substance of knowledge, loving, general, not distinct, or particular, as before. And, therefore, such a soul betaking itself to prayer—like a man with water before him—drinks sweetly without effort, without the necessity of drawing it through the channel of previous reflections, forms, and figures. And the moment such a soul places itself in the presence of God, it makes an act of knowledge, confused, loving, peaceful, and tranquil, wherein it drinks in wisdom, love, and sweetness.

This is the reason why the soul is troubled and disgusted when compelled, in this state, to make meditations and to labour in particular acts of knowledge.

The less such a soul understands, the further does it enter into the night of the spirit, through which it has to pass in order to be united with God, in a way that surpasses all understanding.

§ OBSCURE AND GENERAL KNOWLEDGE

This knowledge is necessary for the abandonment of the way of meditation and reflection. [1]

---

[1] RUYSBROECK : " Thirdly, he must have lost himself in a Way-lessness and in a Darkness, in which all contemplative men wander in fruition and wherein they never again can find themselves in a creaturely way. In the abyss of this darkness, in which the loving spirit had died to itself, there begin the manifestation of God and eternal life. For in this darkness there shines and is born an incomprehensible Light, which is the Son of God, in Whom we behold eternal light."

" Few men can attain to this Divine seeing, because of their own incapacity and the mysteriousness of the light in which one sees."— *The Adornment of the Spiritual Marriage*, Book III.

But it is to be remembered that this general knowledge . . . is at times so subtle and delicate—particularly when most pure, simple, perfect, spiritual, and interior—that the soul, though in the practice thereof, is not observant or conscious of it. This is the case when that knowledge is most pure, clear, and simple, which it is when it enters into a soul most pure and detached from all other acts of knowledge and special perceptions, to which the understanding or the sense may cling. Such a soul, because freed from all those things which were actually and habitually objects of the understanding or of the sense, is not aware of them, because the accustomed objects of sense have failed it. This is the reason why this knowledge, when most pure, perfect, and simple, is the less perceived by the understanding, and is the most obscure.[1]

[1] RUYSBROECK: "At times, the inward man performs his introspection simply, according to the fruitive tendency, above all activity and above all virtues, through a simple inward gazing in the fruition of love. And here he meets God without intermediary. And from out the Divine Unity, there shines into him a simple light; and this light shows him Darkness and Nakedness and Nothingness. In the Darkness, he is enwrapped and falls into somewhat which is in no wise, even as one who has lost his way. In the Nakedness, he loses the perception and discernment of all things, and is transfigured and penetrated by a simple light. In the Nothingness, all his activity fails him; for he is vanquished by the working of God's abysmal love, and in the fruitive inclination of his spirit he vanquishes God, and becomes one spirit with Him. And in this oneness with the Spirit of God, he enters into a fruitive tasting and possesses the Being of God. And he is filled, according to the measure in which he has sunk himself in his essential being, with the abysmal delights and riches of God. And from these riches an envelopment and a plenitude of sensible love flow forth into the unity of the higher powers. And from this plenitude of sensible love, a savoury and penetrating satisfaction flows forth into the heart and the bodily powers. And through this inflow the man becomes immovable within, and helpless as regards himself and all his works. And in the deeps of his ground he knows and feels nothing, in soul or in

So clear is it of all intelligible forms, which are the adequate objects of the understanding, that the understanding is not conscious of its presence. Sometimes, indeed—when it is most pure—it creates darkness, because it withdraws the understanding from its accustomed lights, forms, and fantasies, and then the darkness becomes palpable and visible.

At other times the divine light strikes the soul with such force that the darkness is unfelt and the light unheeded; the soul seems unconscious of all it knows, and is therefore lost, as it were, in forgetfulness, knowing not where it is, nor what has happened to it, unaware of the lapse of time. It

---

body, but a singular radiance with a sensible well-being and an all-pervading savour. This is the first way, and it is the way of emptiness; for it makes a man empty of all things and lifts him up above activity and above all the virtues. And it unites the man with God, and brings about a firm perseverance in the most interior practices which he can cultivate. When, however, any restlessness, or working of the virtues, puts intermediaries, or images, between the inward man and the naked introversion which he desires, then he is hindered in this exercise; for this way consists in a going out, beyond all things, into the Emptiness."—*The Dark Light*, Book II, Chapter LXV.

" Behold, this mysterious brightness, in which one sees everything that one can desire according to the emptiness of the spirit: this brightness is so great that the loving contemplative, in his ground wherein he rests, sees and feels nothing but an incomprehensible Light; and through that Simple Nudity which enfolds all things, he finds himself, and feels himself, to be that same Light by which he sees, and nothing else."—*Op. cit.*, Book III., Chapter II.

" We feel this touch in the unity of our highest powers, above reason, but not without reason, for we understand in truth that we are touched. But if we would know what this is and whence it comes, then reason and all creaturely observation fail."—*Op. cit.*, Book II., Chapter LXIII.

Against the Quietists of his time, Ruysbroeck defined true contemplation as " the supernatural rest, which one possesses in God: for that is a loving self-emergence joined to a simple gazing into the Incomprehensible Brightness."—*The Adornment of Spiritual Marriage*, Book II., Chapter LXVI.

may and does occur that many hours pass while it is in this state of forgetfulness; all seems but a moment when it again returns to itself.

Though he to whose soul is given this knowledge seems to be doing nothing and to be wholly unoccupied, because the imagination has ceased to act, he still should not believe that the time has been lost or uselessly spent: for though the harmonious correspondence of the powers of the soul has ceased, the understanding thereof abides. A sign by which we may discern whether the soul is occupied in this secret intelligence is, that it has no pleasure in the thought of anything high or low.

Still we are not to suppose that this knowledge necessarily induces this forgetfulness; the reality of it does not depend on this. This forgetfulness occurs when God in a special way suspends the faculties of the soul. This does not often occur, for this knowledge does not always fill the whole soul. It is sufficient for the purpose that the understanding should be withdrawn from all particular knowledge, whether temporal or spiritual, and that the will should have no inclination to dwell upon either. This sign serves to show that the soul is in this state of forgetfulness, when this knowledge is furnished and communicated to the understanding only. But when it is communicated to the will also, which is almost always the case in a greater or less degree, the soul cannot but see, if it will reflect thereon, that it is occupied by this knowledge; because it is then conscious of the sweetness of love therein, without any particular knowledge or perception of what it loves.

This is the reason why this knowledge is called loving and general; for as it communicates itself obscurely to the understanding, so also to the will, infusing therein love and sweetness confusedly, without the soul's knowing distinctly the object of its love.

RETURN TO MEDITATION
THE HABIT OF CONTEMPLATION

Here it may be asked, whether proficients, those whom God has begun to lead into this supernatural knowledge of contemplation, are, in virtue of this commencement, never again to return to the way of meditation, reflections, and natural forms? To this I answer, that it is not to be supposed that those who have begun to have this pure and loving knowledge are never to meditate again or attempt it. For in the beginning of their advancement the habit of this is not so perfect as that they should be able at pleasure to perform the acts of it. Neither are they so far advanced beyond the state of meditation as to be unable to meditate and make their reflections as before, and to find therein something new. Yea, rather, at first, when we see, by the help of these signs, that our soul is not occupied in this quiet, or knowledge, it will be necessary to have recourse to reflections, until we attain to the habit of it in some degree of perfection.

Such a degree will be reached when, as often as we apply ourselves to meditation, the soul enters into contemplative peace, without the power or the inclination to meditate. Until we arrive at this, sometimes one method, sometimes the other, occurs in this time of proficiency in such a way that very often the soul finds itself in a loving or peaceful attendance upon God, with all its faculties in repose ; and very often also will find it necessary, for that end, to have recourse to meditation, calmly and with moderation.

When this state is attained to, meditation ceases, and the faculties labour no more ; for then we may rather say, that intelligence and sweetness are wrought in the soul, and that it itself abstains from every effort, except only that it attends lovingly upon God, without any desire to feel or see anything further than to be in the hands of God,[1] Who now communicates Himself to the soul, thus passive, as the light of the sun to him whose eyes are open.

But we must take care if we wish to receive in pureness and abundance this divine light, that no other lights of knowledge, or forms, or figures of meditations, of a more palpable kind, intervene, for nothing of this kind bears any resemblance to that serene and clear light. And, therefore, if at that time we seek to apprehend and reflect on particular objects, however spiritual they may be, we shall obstruct the pure and limpid light of the Spirit, by interposing these clouds before us, as a man who should place anything before his eyes impedes the vision of things beyond.

[1] " Should not my soul, especially during prayer, try to stop all speech, industry, debate, curiosity and the like, and, instead of looking on at what it is doing, what it has done, and what it is going to do, look at God and thus simplify the spirit and empty it of everything and of all care for itself, remaining, in this simple looking at God and at its own nothingness, altogether abandoned to the holy Will of God, in whose operations it must remain quietly content, without being moved in any way to make acts of the will and the understanding ? "—St. Chantal : Letter to St. Francis of Sales.

It appears, then, from all this that the soul, when it shall have purified and emptied itself from all intelligible forms and images, will then dwell in this pure and simple light, transformed thereto in the state of perfection. This light is ever ready to be communicated to the soul, but does not flow in, because of the forms and veils of the creature which infold and embarrass the soul. Take away these hindrances and coverings, as I shall hereafter explain, and the soul in detachment and poverty of spirit will then, being pure and simple, be transformed in the pure and sincere divine Wisdom who is the Son of God. For then that which is natural having failed, that which is divine flows supernaturally into the enamoured soul; for God leaves it not empty without filling it.

When the spiritual man is unable to meditate, let him learn to remain in loving attention to God, in the quiet of his understanding, though he may seem to be doing nothing.

Thus by little and little, and most rapidly, will the divine tranquillity and peace, from this marvellous and deep knowledge of God, involved in the divine love, be infused into his soul.

§ IMAGINARY PERCEPTIONS AND VISIONS

I say, with respect to all impressions and imaginary visions, and others of whatever kind they may be, which present themselves under forms or images, or any particular intelligible forms, whether false as coming from the devil, or known to be true as coming from God, that the understanding is not to perplex itself about them, nor feed itself upon them;

the soul must not willingly accept them, nor rest
upon them, in order that it may be detached, naked,
pure, and sincerely simple, which is the condition of
the divine union.

The chief part of these visions, the spiritual part
infused, eludes the soul's grasp, and is beyond its
comprehension ; the soul cannot discern or explain
it, because it is wholly spiritual. . . . For this cause
I maintain that the soul, passively, without any
intellectual effort, and without knowing how to
make any such effort, receives through these visions
what it can neither understand nor imagine.

These visions will subsequently profit the soul in
the attainment of faith when it shall have perfectly
renounced all that sense and the understanding find
in them ; and when it shall have duly applied
itself to that end which God had in view when
He sent them.

§ PURELY SPIRITUAL PERCEPTIONS
OF THE UNDERSTANDING :
DEFINITIONS

Visions, revelations, locutions, and spiritual impressions—I call these purely spiritual, because they
do not, like those which are bodily and imaginary,
reach the understanding by the way of the senses of
the body ; but because they reach it independently
of every bodily sense, interior or exterior, clearly and
distinctly in a supernatural way, and passively ; that
is, irrespectively of, at least, any active operation on
the part of the soul itself. Speaking generally, we
may say that these four apprehensions may be called

visions of the soul; for we say that the soul sees when it understands.

All which the understanding receives by the way of seeing—for it can see spiritually, as the eyes see bodily—may be called vision; that which it receives by apprehending and perceiving new things, revelation; that which it receives by the way of hearing, locution; and that which it receives in the way of the other senses, such as spiritual odour, taste, and delectation, of which the soul is supernaturally conscious, may be called spiritual impressions. From all this the understanding elicits an act of intelligence or spiritual vision, as I have said, without perceiving any form, image, or figure whatever of the natural imagination or fancy which could furnish any foundation for it: for these things are communicated directly to the soul by a supernatural operation and by supernatural means.

NO ATTACHMENT TO VISIONS

The understanding must be withdrawn from these visions—precisely as from the corporeal and imaginary apprehensions—by being guided and directed in the spiritual night of faith to the divine and substantial union of the love of God, that it may not be embarrassed and made stupid by them, and thereby be hindered on the road of solitude, and detachment necessary for that end. If it be granted that these apprehensions are of a higher kind, more profitable and much more safe than those which are corporeal and imaginary, because they are interior, purely spiritual, and less liable to the intrusions of Satan; still the understanding may be not only

embarrassed by them, but, because of its incautious-
ness, greatly deluded.

§ REVELATIONS

A revelation is nothing else but the disclosure of
some hidden truth, or the manifestation of some
secret or mystery.

KNOWLEDGE OF PURE TRUTHS

This kind of knowledge is twofold : one relates
to the Creator, the other to creatures. And though
both kinds are most full of sweetness, the delight
produced by that which relates to God is not to be
compared with aught beside. . . . This knowledge
relates directly unto God, in the deepest sense of
some of His attributes ; now of His omnipotence,
now of His might, and again of His goodness and
sweetness ; and whenever the soul feels it, it is
penetrated by it. In so far as this becomes pure
contemplation, the soul sees clearly that it cannot
describe it otherwise than in general terms,[1] which
the abundance of delight and happiness forces from
it ; but still those are not adequate expressions of
what it feels within.

This divine knowledge concerning God never

[1] The gift of Intelligence. " Duplex est Dei visio. Una quidem
perfecta, per quam videtur Dei essentia. Alia vero imperfecta, per
quam, etsi non videamus de Deo quid est, videmus tamen quid non
est ; et tanto in hac vita Deum perfectius cognoscimus, quanto magis
intelligimus eum excedere quidquid intellectu comprehenditur. Et
utraque visio pertinet ad donum intellectus."—(S. Thomas, IIa,
IIæ 8, a.7.)

relates to particular things,[1] because it is conversant with the Highest, and therefore cannot be explained unless when it is extended to some truth less than God, which is capable of being described; but this general knowledge is ineffable. It is only a soul in union with God that is capable of this profound loving knowledge, for it is itself that union. This knowledge consists in a certain contact of the soul with the Divinity, and it is God Himself Who is then felt and tasted,[2] though not manifestly and distinctly, as it will be in glory. But this touch of knowledge and of sweetness is so strong and so profound that it penetrates into the inmost substance of the soul.

The devil cannot interfere with it, nor produce anything like it—because there is nothing else comparable with it—nor infuse any sweetness or delight which shall at all resemble it. This knowledge

[1] "As a man raises himself towards Heaven, so this view of the spiritual world becomes simplified and his words fewer; so too when we penetrate into the mystic darkness, not only do our words become more concise but language and thought alike fail us."—DIONYSIUS: *Mystical Theology*, Chapter III.

[2] Gift of Wisdom. "Contactus Dei quo sentitur experimentaliter, et ut objectum conjunctum, etiam antequam videatur intuitive in se, est contactis operationis intimæ, quo operatur intra cor, ita ut sentiatur, et experimentaliter manifestetur, eo quod 'unctio ejus docet nos de omnibus' ut dicitur in 1 Joa. iv.

"Haec cognitio experimentalis datur etiamsi res intuitive non videatur in se; sufficit quod pro proprios effectus quasi per tactum et vivificationem sentiatur."—JOHANNES A S. THOMA, in 1am q. 43, disp. 17.a.

The gift of Wisdom makes us know God by *Union*, by the *invisceration* of God in us, says John of St. Thomas. "Donum sapientiæ habet cognitionem altissimarum causarum, non per quidditatem ipsarum sed per experimentalem quandam unionem et affectivam."—In 1a IIæ q. 70, disp. 18.

"But there is a still more perfect knowledge of God which is the result of a sublime ignorance and which is brought about by virtue of an incomprehensible union."—DIONYSIUS: *Divine Names*, Chapter VII.

savours, in some measure, of the divine essence and of everlasting life, and the devil has no power to simulate anything so great. Nevertheless, the devil is able to produce certain pretended imitations of it, by representing to the soul a certain grandeur and sensible fulness, striving to persuade that this is God; but he cannot so do this as that his influence shall penetrate into the interior part of the soul, renew it, and fill it with love profoundly, as the knowledge of God does. For there are some acts of knowledge and touches of God, wrought by Him in the substance of the soul, which so enrich it that one of them is sufficient, not only to purge away at once certain imperfections, which had hitherto resisted the efforts of a whole life, but also to fill the soul with virtues and divine gifts.

Such is the sweetness and deep delight of these touches of God, that one of them is more than a recompense for all the sufferings of this life, however great their number. They render the soul so generous and so courageous in the endurance of afflictions for God, that it becomes a special pain to see its tribulations diminished.

THESE DIVINE TOUCHES ARE UNEXPECTED; THEIR EFFECTS

Sometimes, when the soul least thinks of it, and when it least desires it, God touches it divinely, causing certain recollections of Himself. Sometimes, too, the divine touches are sudden, occurring even while the soul is occupied with something else, and that occasionally of trifling moment. They are also so sensible and efficacious, that at times they make not only the soul, but the body also, to tremble. At other times they come gently, without any agitation whatever, accompanied by a deep sense of delight and spiritual refreshing. As this knowledge is communicated suddenly and independently of the will, the soul must not strive to receive it, nor strive not to receive it, but be humble and resigned ; for God will do His own work, how and when He will.

I do not say that the soul is to conduct itself negatively here, as in the case of the other apprehensions ; because the divine touches are a part of the union to which I would direct the soul, and for attaining unto which I teach it to withdraw and detach itself from all besides. The means by which God effects this great work must be humility and patient suffering for love of Him, with resignation, and indifference as to all reward. These graces are not bestowed on the soul which cleaves to anything of its own, inasmuch as they are wrought by an especial love of God towards the soul, which also loves Him in perfect detachment and pure disinterestedness.

THE GREAT INSIGHT OF PURIFIED SOULS

Perfect persons, or those who are advancing to perfection, very frequently receive the knowledge of things present or distant, in a certain illumination of their purified and enlightened mind.

Those persons, whose minds are purified, ascertain with great facility, some better than others, what is passing in the hearts of men, their inclinations and their capacities ; and this from certain outward signs, however slight they may be, such as expressions, motions, or gestures.

Therefore, though spiritual men cannot, in the order of nature, know the thoughts and intentions of others, yet by supernatural enlightenment, through certain signs, they may well do so. And though they may be often deceived in their interpretation of these signs, yet for the most part they will be correct. But we are not to rely on any of these means, for the devil may insinuate herein with exceeding cunning, and in consequence of this, we must renounce this method and form of knowledge.

§ INTERIOR LOCUTIONS

I. SUCCESSIVE

At all times when successive words take place, it is when the mind is collected and absorbed by some particular subject; and while attentively considering the matter which occupies its thoughts, it proceeds from one part of it to another, puts words and reasonings together so much to the purpose, and with such facility and clearness discovers by reflection things it knew not before, that it seems to itself as if it was not itself which did so, but some third person which addressed it interiorly, reasoning, answering, and informing. And in truth there is good ground for such a notion; the mind then reasons with itself as one man does with another, and to a certain extent it is so. For though it be the mind itself that thus reasons, yet the Holy Ghost very often assists it in the formation of these conceptions, words, and reasonings. . . . This is one way in which the Holy Ghost teaches us.

Now, though it is true that there can be no illusion in this communication, and in the enlightenment of the understanding, still illusions may, and do, frequently occur in the formal words and reasonings which the understanding forms about them. . . . When a man has the clue of a true principle and then deals with it by his own abilities, or in the ignorance of his weak understanding, it is an easy thing for such an one to fall into delusions . . . the Holy Ghost enlightens the recollected understanding, and in proportion to its recollection; and, as there can be no greater recollection of the understanding than in faith, the Holy Ghost will not enlighten it in any other way more than in that of faith.

By the understanding the soul may receive the knowledge of one, two, or three truths; but by faith the Wisdom of God generally, which is His Son, in one simple universal knowledge.

If the soul occupies itself with matters evident and of little moment, it is kept from the communication of the abyss of faith, wherein God supernaturally and secretly teaches the soul, and trains it up, in a way it knows not, in virtues and in graces.

There are some men whose understanding is so quick and penetrating that their conceptions, when they are self-recollected, naturally proceed with great facility, and form themselves into these locutions and reasonings so clearly as to make them think that God is speaking. But it is not so. All this is the work of the understanding. . . .

These interior successive locutions furnish occasions to the evil spirit, especially when persons have an inclination or affection for them. Such is his dealing with those who have entered into a compact with him, tacit or expressed. Thus he converses with some heretics, especially with heresiarchs; he informs their understanding with most subtle thoughts and reasonings.

It appears, then, that these successive words may proceed from three sources: from the Holy Spirit, moving and enlightening; from the natural light of the understanding; and from the evil spirit suggesting. It will be rather a difficult matter to describe the signs and tokens, by which it may be known from which of these sources particular locutions proceed, but some general notions may be given.

When the soul loves, and at the same time is humbly and reverently conscious of that love, it is a sign that these locutions come from the Holy Ghost, Who, whenever He grants us these graces, grants them through love.

When they come from the vivacity and light of the understanding only, it is that which affects them without any operation of virtue—though the will may love naturally in the knowledge and light of those truths—and, when the meditation is over, the will remains cold, though not inclined to vanity or evil, unless the devil shall have tempted us anew. The locutions of the Holy Ghost cannot issue in this, for, when they are over, the will is usually affectionately disposed towards God, and inclined to good, though sometimes, certainly, the will may be dry, even after the communications of the Holy Spirit, God thus ordering it for the profit of particular souls. At other times, too, the soul will not be very sensible of the operations or motions of these virtues, and yet what passes within will have been good. This is why I have said that it is sometimes difficult to distinguish one from another, because of the various effects which they sometimes have.

The evil locutions are occasionally hard to distinguish, for, though they dry up the love of God in the will, and incline men to vanity, self-esteem, or complacency, still they beget at times a certain false humility and fervent affection of the will founded on self-love, which requires for its detection great spirituality of mind.

II. FORMAL LOCUTIONS

The second kind of interior locutions are formal words, uttered in the mind. . . . I call these formal words, because the mind formally perceives they are spoken by a third person, independently of its own operations. For this reason they are very different from those of which I have just spoken.

The locutions of which I am now speaking are sometimes perfectly formed, sometimes not. . . . Sometimes it is one word, at another two or more. . . . Still all takes place without the active participation of the mind, for it is as if another person were then speaking. . . . They do not always remove a certain repugnance which the soul feels, but rather increase it; and this is the operation of God, the end of which is the more perfect instruction, humiliation, and profit of the soul. This repugnance is in general the result, when great and noble deeds are commanded; and there is greater promptitude and facility, when vile and humiliating things are enjoined.

On the other hand, when these locutions are from the evil spirit, great things are readily undertaken, but humble occupations become repugnant.

We must not make much of these formal locutions any more than of the successive. For over and above the occupation of the mind with that which is not the legitimate and proximate means of union with God, namely faith, there is also the too certain risk of diabolical delusions. We can scarcely distinguish at times what locutions come from a good, and what from an evil, spirit. And as the effects of them are not great we can hardly distinguish them by that test; for sometimes the diabolic locutions have a more sensible influence on the imperfect, than the divine locutions on spiritual persons. We must, also, not obey them at once, whether they come from a good or evil spirit. But we must not neglect to manifest them to a prudent confessor, or to some discreet and learned person, who shall teach us, and decide for us, what we ought to do; and when we have had his decision, we must be resigned and indifferent in the matter.

III. SUBSTANTIAL LOCUTIONS

The third kind of interior locutions are the substantial words. Though these are also formal, inasmuch as they are formally impressed on the soul, they differ from them in this; the substantial locutions produce a vivid and substantial effect in the soul, while those locutions which are only formal do not, though it be true that every substantial locution is also formal, yet every formal locution is not substantial; but only that which really impresses on the soul what it signifies. One locution of God does for the soul far more at once than that soul has done for itself in its whole past life.

The soul is not called upon to do or attempt anything with regard to these locutions, but to be resigned and humble. It is not called upon to undervalue or fear them, nor to labour in doing what they enjoined it. For God by means of these substantial locutions works in and by the soul Himself. And herein they differ from the formal and successive locutions. The soul need not reject these locutions, for the effect of them remains substantially in the soul, and full of blessing; and therefore the action of the soul is useless, because it has received them passively. . . .

The devil cannot passively produce this substantial effect in any soul whatever, so as to impress upon it the effect and habit of his locution; though he may, by his suggestions, lead those souls in whom he dwells as their lord, in virtue of their voluntary compact with him, to perform deeds of exceeding malignity. Thus the substantial locutions conduce greatly to the union of the soul with God; and the more interior they are, the more substantial are they and the more profitable.

§ SPIRITUAL IMPRESSIONS

Spiritual impressions are frequently effected supernaturally in spiritual men.

There are two kinds of these distinct spiritual impressions. The first kind is in the affection of

the will, the second . . . seems to have been
wrought in the very substance of the soul. Both
the one and the other are extremely diversified. The
first, when from God, is very high; but the second
is the highest, of great profit and advantage.

God sends them to whom, and why, He wills.
Sometimes a person who has done many good works
will never have these touches, and another of less
merit, will have them most profoundly and most
abundantly. It is not necessary, therefore, for the
soul to be actually occupied with spiritual things—
though that is the better state—in order to be the
object of the divine touches, of which these impressions are the result, for they frequently occur when
the soul is heedless of them. Some of these touches
are distinct, and pass rapidly away; others less so,
but of longer continuance.

We must, therefore, remember that, from all these
impressions, whether the divine touches which cause
them be rapid, or continuous and successive, there
flows frequently into the understanding the apprehension of knowledge or intelligence; which is
usually a most profound and sweet sense of God, to
which, as well as to the impression from which it
flows, no name can be given. This knowledge
comes, sometimes in one way, sometimes in another,
now most deep and clear, again less so, according to
the nature of the divine touches, which occasion the
impressions, and according to the nature of the
impressions, of which it is the result.

It is not necessary to waste words here in caution-
ing and directing the understanding, amid this
knowledge, in faith to the divine union. For as

these impressions are passively wrought in the soul, without any co-operation on its part, so also the knowledge which results from them is passively received in the understanding . . . the understanding ought not to meddle with them, but remain passive, inclining the will to consent freely and gratefully, and not interfering itself. . . .

Let the soul be resigned, humble, and passive, for as it receives passively from God this knowledge, so will He communicate it, of His own good pleasure, when He sees it humble and detached. By so living, the soul will put no obstacles in the way of the profitableness of this knowledge for the divine union : and that profitableness is great. All these touches are touches of union, which is passively effected in the soul.

BOOK III

PURGATION AND ACTIVE NIGHT OF THE MEMORY AND THE WILL

PART I

I. THE MEMORY AND NATURAL PERCEPTIONS

ANSWER TO A DOUBT AS TO THE EMPTYING
OF THE FACULTIES

WHEN the reader observes that I teach the annihilation of the understanding, the memory and the will in the matter of their operations, he will perhaps imagine that I am destroying, and not building up, the spiritual edifice. This objection would be valid, if my purpose here was to instruct only beginners, who are to be led onwards by means of these discursive and tangible apprehensions. But as I am teaching how to advance by contemplation to the divine union—for which end all these means, and the sensible exertion of the powers of the soul must cease and be silent, in order that God in His own way may bring that union to pass—it is necessary to release the faculties and to empty them, and to make them renounce their natural jurisdiction and operations, in order that the supernatural may fill and enlighten them . . . as it is most true that the soul knoweth God, rather by what He is not, than by what He is, it follows of necessity that if we are to draw near unto Him, it must be by denying and renouncing to the uttermost all that may be denied, of our apprehensions, natural and supernatural alike.

THE STRIPPING OF THE MEMORY

The natural knowledge of the memory is all that knowledge it can form about the objects of the five bodily senses : hearing, seeing, smelling, tasting and touching, and all else of the like kind. The memory must be stripped and emptied of all this knowledge and of these forms ; it must labour to destroy all sense of them, so that no impression whatever of them shall be left behind ; it must forget them, and withdraw itself from them, and that as completely as if they had never entered into it. Nothing less than the annihilation of the memory as to all these forms will serve, if it is to be united with God. For that union can never take place without a total separation from these forms which are not God, for God is without form ; neither is He the object of any distinct knowledge whatever.

UNION EMPTIES THE MEMORY

As God is without form or image, on which the memory may dwell, so when the memory is united with God—as we see by daily experience—it remains without form or figure, with the imagination suppressed, and itself absorbed in supreme felicity, in profound oblivion, remembering nothing. The divine union expels every fancy, and shuts out all forms and knowledge ; it raises the memory to that which is supernatural, leaving it in such deep forgetfulness that it must do violence to itself, if it will remember anything at all. Such at times is this forgetfulness of the memory, and suspension of the imaginative powers, because of the union of the memory with God, that time passes by unheeded, and what took place in the interval cannot be known. If God is to bring about this perfect union, memory must be severed from all acts of knowledge of which it is capable. But it is to be observed, that this suspension never occurs thus in those who are perfect, because they have attained already to the perfect union, and this suspension is related to the commencement of that state.

FIRST OBJECTION :

WHAT IS LEFT OF MAN ?[1]

To this I reply: the more the memory is united to God the more it loses all distinct knowledge, and at last all such fades utterly away, when the state of perfection is reached. In the beginning, when this is going on, great forgetfulness ensues, for these forms and knowledge fall into oblivion, men neglect themselves in outward things, forgetting to eat or drink; they do not remember whether they have done or left undone a particular work, whether they have seen such things or not, or whether such and such things have been mentioned to them; and all this because the memory is lost in God.

But he who has attained to the habit of union does

---

[1] TAULER : " But I will be asked : ' Then what does the soul attach itself to, if it rejects every kind of image in this way ? ' It attaches to nothing whatsoever, and stays naked and isolated, for if it rested on anything, that thing would necessarily be some image. It takes, then, for its share the sufferings and the cross of love."—*Institutions*, Chapter XXXV.

not forget, in this way, that which relates to moral and natural reason ; he performs in much greater perfection all necessary and befitting actions, though by the ministry of forms and knowledge, in the memory, supplied in a special manner by God. In the state of union, which is a supernatural state, the memory and the other faculties fail as to their natural functions, and rise beyond their natural objects upwards unto God.

And thus, then, when the memory is transformed in God, no permanent forms or knowledge can be impressed upon it ; the operations of the memory, therefore, and of the other powers in this state are, as it were, divine ; God has entered into possession, by this transformation, as their absolute Lord ; guides and governs them Himself divinely by His own spirit and will, as it is written, " He who is joined to the Lord is one spirit ; " and therefore the operations of the soul in the state of union are the operations of the Holy Ghost, and, consequently, divine.

Now, the actions of such souls are only what they ought to be, and reasonable, and not what they ought not to be : because under the influence of the Holy Ghost they know what they ought to know, are ignorant of what they ought to be ignorant, remember what they ought to remember, forget what they ought to forget, love what they ought to love, and love not that which is not God. Thus in general the first motions of the faculties of these souls are, as it were, divine. . . . The actions and the prayers of souls in a state of union always attain their end.

SECOND OBJECTION :

SO COMPLETE A PURIFICATION IS IMPOSSIBLE

God must raise the soul up into this supernatural state ; but the soul, so far as it can, must also be in good dispositions, which it may acquire by the help which God supplies. And so when the soul rejects these forms and empties itself of them, God causes it to enter into the enjoyment of this union. When God does this, the soul is passive, as I shall explain in speaking of the passive night ; and He will then bestow upon it the habit of perfect union, proportional to its good dispositions, when it shall seem to Him good to do so.

The spiritual man must observe this precaution : never to treasure up or retain in the memory anything he may see, hear, taste, touch, or smell ; but to let them pass away, forgetting them, and never reflecting upon them, unless when it may be necessary to do so in order to a good meditation.

If for a time this forgetfulness of all knowledge and forms is not felt to be profitable, the spiritual man must not therefore grow wearied ; for God will draw near in His own time, and for so great a blessing we ought to wait long, and patiently persevere in hope.

THIRD OBJECTION :

THE SOUL WILL BE DEPRIVED OF GOOD THOUGHTS

You will further object, and say, that the soul thus deprives itself of many good thoughts and meditations about God, which are most profitable to it in the blessings they bring with them.

I answer, all that is purely God and promotes this pure simple general and confused knowledge, is not to be rejected, but only what detains the memory on images, forms, figures, and similitudes of created things. And in order that God may accomplish this purgation, pureness of soul is most profitable— that pureness which consists in not setting the affections thereof on any created or transitory things, and in not regarding them; for, in my opinion, the opposite conduct will not fail to make a deep impression because of the imperfection which cleaves to the powers of the soul in their operation. It is, therefore, much better to impose silence on the faculties, that God may speak. In order to attain to this state, the natural operations must cease. This takes place, as the prophet saith, when the soul comes into solitude with its faculties, and when God speaks to the heart: " I . . . will lead her into the wilderness, and I will speak to her heart." [1]

FOURTH OBJECTION :

THE SOUL WILL BE GIVEN TO DISTRACTION

But if you still object and say, that the soul will profit nothing, if the memory does not reflect and dwell upon God, and that it will be liable to much lukewarmness and distraction—I answer, it is impossible; for if the memory be entirely withdrawn from the things of this life and of the next, no evil, no distraction, no folly or vice can enter within it. . . . This certainly would be the case, if

[1] Os. ii. 14.

we opened the door to the consideration of earthly things, while it is shut against that of heavenly things : but we shut the door against everything which is prejudicial to union, and out of which distractions may come, bringing the memory into silence, that the Spirit only may be heard.

Let the soul, therefore, be " enclosed " without anxiety or alarm ; and He Who, when the doors were shut, entered bodily in among His disciples, and said, " Peace be unto you," in an unexpected and inconceivable way, will enter spiritually into the soul without its knowledge or co-operation, when it keeps the doors of its powers closed—the memory, understanding, and will—and fill it with His peace, turning into it the river of peace. . . . And he will take away all misgivings, and suspicions, all uneasiness and darkness, which made the soul afraid that it was already, or on the point of being, lost.

Be, therefore, earnest in prayer, and hope in detachment and emptiness ; thy good will not tarry.

POWERLESSNESS OF THE DEVIL
BEFORE THIS EMPTINESS

The devil can . . . infect the soul with pride, avarice, envy, and hatred. He can also excite unjust enmities, vain love, and delude us in many ways.

Now, if the memory were blind to these things, and annihilated in forgetfulness of them, it would shut the door against the evil spirit, so far as this evil is concerned, and free itself wholly from these things, which would be a great blessing. The evil spirit cannot molest the soul but through the operations of its faculties, and chiefly by the help of forms and fancies : for upon these depend, more or less, all the operations of the other faculties. And therefore, if the memory annihilates itself as to them, the devil can do nothing ; because he can find nothing to lay hold of, and without something of that kind he can do nothing whatever.

This emptying of the memory, though the advantages of it are not so great as those of the state of union, yet, merely because it delivers souls from much sorrow, grief, and sadness, besides imperfections and sins, is in itself a great good.

This is a truth of daily experience : whenever the soul broods over anything, it is changed or disturbed, be it much or little, according to the measure of its apprehension.

THIS EMPTINESS PREVENTS DISQUIETUDE AND GIVES PEACE

Disquietude is always vanity, because it serves no good. Yea, even if the whole world were thrown into confusion, and all things in it, disquietude on that account is vanity, for it hurts us more than it relieves us. To endure all things, with an equable and peaceful mind, not only brings with it many blessings to the soul, but it also enables us, in the midst of our difficulties, to have a clear judgment about them, and to minister the fitting remedy for them.

This peace of mind no man will ever lose, if only he will forget his own notions and cast aside his thoughts, and withdraw from the sight, and hearing, and discussion of matters, so far as it is possible for him. We are naturally so frail and weak, that, in spite of all self-discipline, we can scarcely avoid stumbling on the recollection of many things, which disturb and disquiet our mind ; though it may have been once established in peace and tranquillity, oblivious of all things.

§ MEMORY AND SUPERNATURAL APPREHENSIONS (VISIONS, REVELATIONS, INTERIOR LOCUTIONS, SUPERNATURAL PERCEPTIONS)

In order to attain the blessing of union, the soul must never reflect upon those objects which have been clearly and distinctly present to it in a supernatural way. We must always keep this principle before our eyes ; the more the soul attends to any clear and distinct apprehension, natural or supernatural, the less will be its capacity and disposition for entering into the abyss of faith, wherein all things else are absorbed. The more the memory divests itself, the greater its hope ; and the greater its hope, the greater its union with God. For with respect to God, the more the soul hopes, the more it obtains, and it then hopes most when it is most divested ; and when it shall be perfectly divested, it will then have the possession of God, such as is possible on earth in the divine union.

HARM DONE BY ATTACHMENT TO SUPERNATURAL PERCEPTIONS

(1) Frequent illusions, mistaking one thing for another.

(2) Proximate occasions of presumption or vain glory.

(3) Opportunities of deceiving, which they furnish to the devil.

(4) Hindrance to union with God in hope.

(5) Low views of God for the most part.

He who shall perplex his memory and the other powers of his soul with matters that they can comprehend, will never think and feel about God as he ought to do.

THE NATURAL ACTION OF THE SOUL
IS A HINDRANCE

If the soul exerts itself its action will be only natural, or, at the utmost, if supernatural, far inferior to that which God wills. In its own strength the soul cannot do more, seeing that it neither does, nor can, influence itself supernaturally; it is God that so influences it, but with its own consent. If, then, the soul will do anything itself, it will, necessarily, so far as itself is concerned, hinder the communication of God, that is, the Spirit; because it has recourse to its own operations, which are of another kind and far inferior to those of God. This, then, is to extinguish the Spirit.

§ MEMORY AND SPIRITUAL APPREHENSIONS

The nature of this knowledge, and the conduct to be observed by the soul with reference to it, in order to be united with God, has been sufficiently explained in the twenty-fourth chapter of the second book.[1] As to the knowledge of the uncreated perfections, that may be remembered as often as we

[1] Cf. *supra*, p. 52.

can, for it will produce great results ; for that is, as I said before, touches and impressions of the divine union towards which I am directing the soul.

HOW THE SOUL MUST ACT

What we have to do, then, in order to live in the simple and perfect hope of God, whenever these forms, knowledge, and distinct images occur, is not to fix our minds upon them, but to turn immediately to God, emptying the memory of all such matters, in loving affection.

PART II

THE WILL

WE have done nothing . . . if we have not purified the will in the order of charity, which is the third theological virtue.

I. TEMPORAL GOODS

By these I mean riches, rank, office, and other dignities; children, relations, and alliances. . . .

Even in this life, for one joy denied through love of Him and for the sake of evangelical perfection, God will give a hundredfold, according to His promise.

II. NATURAL GOODS

By natural goods I mean beauty, grace, comeliness, bodily constitution, and all other physical endowments, and also good understanding, discretion, and other rational qualities. He who is thus endowed, ought to be very cautious, and watchful in his conduct, lest he should furnish another with the opportunity of withdrawing his heart from God even for a moment. For these natural gifts and graces are so prolific in temptations and in occasions of sin, as well to the owner as to the beholder, that scarcely any one can avoid all entanglement of the heart in them. When our affections, free from the influence of natural goods, which are deceitful, rest upon no one, the soul is free to love all men reasonably and spiritually, as God wills them to be loved. No one deserves to be loved except for his goodness, and when we love in this way, our love is pleasing unto God, and in great liberty, and if there be attachment in it there is greater attachment to God. For then the more this love grows, the more also grows our love of God, and the deeper our love of Him the more we shall love our neighbour : for the principle of both is the same.

III. SENSIBLE GOODS

By sensible goods I mean all that is cognisable by the senses, of sight, of hearing, of smell, of taste and of touch, and of the interior working of the imaginative powers ; all of which belong to the interior and exterior bodily senses. Whenever, in hearing music, or other agreeable sounds, in smelling sweet odours, in tasting what is delicious, in touching what is soothing, the affections of the will rise consciously in an instant unto God, and that movement gives us more pleasure than the sensible occasion of it, and when we have no pleasure in that cause, but because of its effects, that is a sign of profit, and shows that the objects of sense minister unto the spirit. In this way we may use them, for now they subserve that end for which God hath made them ; namely, that He may be the better known and loved on their account. For as all that our first parents said and did in the state of innocence in paradise furnished them with means of sweeter contemplation, because their sensual nature was ordered by, and subject unto, reason, so he also whose senses are subject to the spirit and purged from all sensible objects, in their first motions, elicits delight of sweet knowledge and contemplation of God.

From these considerations I come to this conclusion, that, until we have so habituated our senses to this purgation from sensible joy, as to have obtained the benefit of which I have spoken, namely, that instant movement upwards to God, we still need to deny ourselves in all joy, that we may wean our soul from the life of sense.

There will be an increase of essential glory, corresponding to their love of God, for those who have left all things for Him ; because every momentary and fleeting joy, which we now deny, will, as St. Paul has said, work in us eternally an infinite weight of glory.

IV. MORAL GOODS

The fourth kind of goods in which the will rejoices are moral goods. By these I mean virtues, the moral habits of them, the practice of any virtue whatever, works of mercy, keeping the law of God and of the state, good dispositions and temper.

A Christian ought to rejoice, not because of his good works and virtuous life, but because his life and acts are such solely for the love of God, and for no other reason whatever. God will not reward them for their good works, because they seek it here in this world, in the joy, or the comfort, or the honourable advantages of their good works ; of them our Saviour saith, " Amen. I say to you, they have received their reward."[1]

V. SUPERNATURAL GOODS

By these I mean all those gifts and graces of God, which surpass our natural powers and capacities, called by theologians *gratis datæ* :—such as the gifts of " wisdom and understanding " given to Solomon, and those mentioned by St. Paul, namely, " faith, the grace of healing, working of miracles, prophecy, the knowledge and discerning of spirits, the interpretation of words, and also the gift of tongues."[2] . . . These gifts, in the use of them, have an immediate reference to the edification of men, and are given by God for that special end. Moreover, they may be wrought by persons not in a state of grace and of charity. . . . Many men who have thought much of their own good works, when asking to be admitted unto His glory, will say, " Have not we prophesied in Thy name . . . and done many miracles in Thy name ? " Christ our Redeemer will answer : " Depart from Me, you that work iniquity."

He who is supernaturally endowed ought, therefore, to cleanse himself from all desire of, and from all joy in, the exercise of his supernatural gifts ; and God, Who gives them supernaturally for the edification of the Church in general, or of its members in particular, will also supernaturally direct him in the use of them, in the right way and at the right time. As He commanded His disciples to take no thought beforehand how or what they should speak,[3] that

[1] S. Matth. vi. 2.   [2] 1 Cor. xii. 9 10.   [3] S. Mark xiii. 11.

being a supernatural act of faith, so also is it His will—the use of these gifts being of not less importance—that man should bide His time, because the exercise of these gifts is to depend upon His will. Thus the disciples, in whom these gifts and graces were infused, prayed God, nevertheless, to put forth His hand, that they might work miracles and heal the sick and thereby plant the faith of Jesus Christ our Lord in the hearts of men.[1]

When men attach much importance to miracles, they depart from the substantial exercise of faith, which is an obscure habit; and thus where signs and miracles abound, there is the less merit in believing. "Faith has no merit," saith S. Gregory the Great, "where human reason supplies proof."[2] For this reason did God work many signs, before He showed Himself to His disciples; that they might believe without seeing, and so not lose the merit of faith in His resurrection, which they would have done had they seen Him first.

As God is exalted when our joy is grounded on our detachment from all things, much more is He exalted when we refrain from joy in His most marvellous works to place it in Him alone; for these graces are of a higher nature by reason of their supernatural character, and therefore to detach ourselves from them to rejoice in God alone, is to give greater honour and glory to God than to them; for the more numerous and important are the things we disregard for the sake of another, the more we esteem and magnify Him.

[1] Acts iv. 29–30. [2] Hom. 26, in Evangel.

VI. SPIRITUAL GOODS

There are people who, because of their want of knowledge, make use of spiritual things in the order of sense only, leaving the spirit empty . . . by spiritual goods I mean all those that move us and help us in divine things, in the intercourse of the soul with God, and in the communications of God to the soul.

Having said before how the understanding and the memory are to be directed amid such and such apprehensions to the divine union, and that the same applies to the will also, it is not necessary to return to the subject here. . . .

What I have already said of emptying the memory and the understanding of all their apprehensions is applicable to the will; for seeing that the understanding and the other powers cannot admit or reject without the intervention of the will, it is clear that the same principle applies to the one as well as to the other. Every explanation, therefore, that the subject requires may be found above (cf. pp. 63–74), for all the evils and dangers there enumerated will befall the soul if it does not refer unto God all the joy of the will in these apprehensions.

HOLY IMAGES

A devout man grounds his devotion chiefly on the invisible; he requires but few images, and uses but few. Be assured of this, the more the soul clings to images or sensible motives the less will its devotion and prayers ascend upwards unto God. When God grants graces, and works miracles, He does so, in general, through images not very well made, nor artistically painted or adorned, so that the faithful may attribute nothing to the work of the artist.

And very often our Lord grants His graces by means of images in remote and solitary places. In remote places, that the pilgrimage to them may stir up our devotion, and make it the more intense. In solitary places, that we may retire from the noise and concourse of men to pray in solitude, like our Lord Himself. He, therefore, who goes on a pilgrimage, will do well to do so when others do not, even at an unusual time. When many people make a pilgrimage, I would advise staying at home, for, in general, men return more dissipated than they were before.

ORATORIES

As to the use of special places for prayer and the like, I may observe that it is lawful, and even expedient, for beginners to feel a sensible pleasure in images, oratories, and other visible objects of devotion. . . . But the spiritual man, if he is to advance, must deny himself in all those tastes and desires in which the will has pleasure, for true spirituality has but slight connection with any of these things, inasmuch as it consists solely in interior recollection and mental converse with God. For though the spiritual man makes use of images and oratories, yet it is only as it were in passing, and the mind at once rests in God, forgetting all sensible objects.

In this matter of intimate intercourse with God, that place ought to be chosen which least occupies and allures the senses. It must, therefore, not be a place agreeable and delightful to sense, such as some people search for, lest instead of serving to recollection of mind, it minister to the recreation and satisfactions of sense. For this end, it is well to make choice of a solitary and even wild spot, so that the mind may ascend firmly and directly to God, without hindrance or detention on the part of visible things. . . . For this reason our Saviour commonly chose to pray in solitary places, where there were no attractions for the senses—herein giving us an example —but places which tended to lift up the soul to God, such as mountains, which are elevated spots, and generally barren, furnishing no resources for sensible recreation.

He, therefore, who is truly spiritual looks only to interior recollection in oblivion of all things, and for that end chooses a place that is most free from all sensible sweetness and attractions, withdrawing his thoughts from all that surrounds him, so that in the absence of created things, he may rejoice in God alone.

For if the soul becomes habituated to the sweetness of sensible devotion, it will never advance to the power of spiritual joy which is to be found in spiritual detachment by means of interior recollection.

THE DARK NIGHT OF THE SOUL

BOOK I

THE PASSIVE NIGHT OF SENSE

THE NECESSITY OF THIS NIGHT FOR BEGINNERS IN CONTEMPLATION

Souls begin to enter the dark night when God is drawing them out of the state of beginners, which is that of those who meditate on the spiritual road, and is leading them into that of proficients, the state of contemplatives, that, having passed through it, they may arrive at the state of the perfect, which is that of the divine union with God.

GENERAL IMPERFECTIONS OF BEGINNERS
LOVE OF CONSOLATIONS

Such souls delight to spend many hours, and perhaps whole nights, in prayer; their pleasures are penances, their joy in fasting, and their consolations lie in the use of the sacraments and in speaking of divine things. For many persons, spirituality consists in remaining faithful to practices thus understood; and, not without good effect, they put into them all the care and all the diligence necessary. Nevertheless, in the true spiritual sense, what they do is very weak and very imperfect. They are drawn to these things and to their spiritual exercises by the comfort and satisfaction they find therein.

. . . In these very spiritual works themselves they commit faults and fall into many imperfections.

SPIRITUAL IMPERFECTIONS OF BEGINNERS
I. PRIDE

When beginners become aware of their own fervour and diligence in their spiritual works and devotional exercises, this prosperity of theirs gives rise to secret pride—though holy things tend of their own nature to humility—because of their imperfections ; and the issue is that they conceive a certain satisfaction in the contemplation of their works and of themselves. From the same source, too, proceeds that empty eagerness which they display to some extent, and occasionally very much, in speaking before others of the spiritual life, and sometimes as teachers rather than learners. They condemn others in their heart when they see that they are not devout in their way. Sometimes also they say it in words, showing themselves herein to be like the Pharisee, who in the act of prayer boasted of his own works and despised the Publican.

Some of them go so far as to desire none should be thought good but themselves, and so, at all times both in word and deed fall into condemnation and detraction of others. They are occasionally desirous that others should perceive their spirituality and devotion, and for that end they give outward tokens by movements, sighs and divers ceremonies ; sometimes, too, they fall into certain trances in public rather than in private—whereto Satan contributes—and are pleased when others are witnesses of them.

They are ashamed to confess their sins plainly,

lest their confessors should think less of them, so they go about palliating them, that they may not seem so bad ; which is excusing rather than accusing themselves. Sometimes they go to a stranger to confess their sins that their usual confessor may think they are not sinners, but good people.

Scarcely anyone can be found who, in his first fervours, did not fall into some of these faults.

But those who at this time are going on to perfection proceed in a very different way, and in a very different temper of mind : they grow and are built up in humility.

For the greater their fervour, the more numerous their good works ; and the keener the pleasure therein, the more they perceive—for they humble themselves—how much is that which God deserves at their hands, and how little is all they can do for Him ; thus the more they do, the less are they satisfied. They have a great desire to speak of their shortcomings and sins, which they would rather have known than their virtues. When they fall into any imperfection they bear up under it with humility, in meekness of spirit, in loving fear of God, and hoping in Him. But the souls who in the beginning travel thus towards perfection are, as I said, few, yea, very few.

II. SPIRITUAL AVARICE.

Many a beginner also falls at times into great spiritual avarice. Scarcely anyone· is contented with that measure of the spirit which God gives ; they are very disconsolate and querulous because they do not find the comfort they desire in spiritual things. Many are never satisfied with listening to spiritual counsels and precepts, with reading books which treat of their state; and they spend more time in this than in doing their duty, having no regard to that mortification, and perfection of interior poverty of spirit to which they ought to apply themselves. Besides, they load themselves with images, rosaries, and crucifixes, curious and costly.

III. TENDENCY TO SENSUALITY

Very often, in the midst of their spiritual exercises, and when they cannot help themselves, the impure movements and disturbances of sensuality are felt; and sometimes even when the mind is absorbed in prayer, or when they are receiving the sacraments of penance and the eucharist. These movements, not being in their power, proceed from one of three sources.

(i.) They proceed occasionally—though but rarely, and in persons of delicate constitutions— from sensible sweetness in spiritual things. For when sense and spirit are both delighted together, the whole nature of man is moved in that delectation according to its measure and character. For then the spirit, that is, the higher part of our nature, is moved to delight itself in God; and sensuality, which is the lower part, is moved towards sensible gratification, because it knows, and admits, of none other, and therefore is moved to what lies nearest to it, namely, sensual pleasure. And so it happens that the soul is in spirit praying, and on the other hand in the senses troubled, to its great disgust, with the rebellious movements and disturbances of the flesh passively; this happens often at the moment of communion.

(ii.) Satan, in order to disquiet the soul during prayer, or when preparing for it, causes these filthy movements of our lower nature, and these, when in any degree admitted, are injury enough. Some persons not only relax in their prayers through fear of these movements, which is the object of Satan when he undertakes to assail them, but even abandon them altogether, for they imagine· that they are more liable to these assaults during prayer than at other times. This is certainly true; for the devil then assails them more than at other times, that they may cease from prayer. He represents before them then, most vividly, the most foul and filthy images.

(iii.) The third source of these depraved movements which war against the soul is usually the fear of them.

Some souls are so sensitive that they never experience spiritual fervour or consolation in prayer without the spirit of luxury intruding.

Sometimes, spiritual persons, when either speaking of spiritual things, or doing good works, display a certain energy or boldness towards persons whom they may call to mind or encounter, making before these a display of a certain measure of vain joy.

Some, too, form spiritual friendships with others, the source of which is luxury, and not spirituality. We may know it to be so by observing whether the remembrance of that affection increases our recollection and love of God, or brings remorse of conscience. When this affection is purely spiritual, the love of God grows with it, and the more we think of it the more we think of God, and the greater our longing for Him; for the one grows with the other.

When the soul enters the dark night, these affections are ruled by reason; that night strengthens and purifies the affection which is according to God, and removes, destroys, or mortifies the other. In the beginning both are by it put out of sight, as I shall explain hereafter.

IV. ANGER

When spiritual things give beginners no more sweetness and delight, they naturally become peevish, and in that bitterness of spirit prove a burden to themselves in all they do; trifles make them angry, and they are at times intolerable to all about them. This happens generally after great sweetness in prayer; and so, when that sensible sweetness is past, their natural temper is soured and rendered morose. They are like a babe weaned from the breast, which he found so sweet. When this natural feeling of displeasure is not permitted to grow, there is no sin, but only imperfection, which will have to be purged away in the severity and aridities of the dark night.

There are other spiritual persons, too, among these who fall into another kind of spiritual anger. They are angry with other people for their faults, with a sort of unquiet zeal, and watch them; they are occasionally moved to blame them, and even do so in anger, constituting themselves guardians of virtue. All this is contrary to spiritual meekness.

Others, again, seeing their own imperfections, become angry with themselves with an impatience that is not humble. They are so impatient with their shortcomings as if they would be saints in one day. . . . There is no perfect remedy for this but in the dark night. There are, however, some people who are so patient, and who advance so slowly in their spiritual progress, that God wishes they were not so patient.

V. SPIRITUAL GLUTTONY

There is scarcely one among beginners, however good his progress, who, in the matter of this sin, does not fall into some of the many imperfections to which beginners are liable, because of that sweetness which in the beginning they find in spiritual exercises.

For, allured by the delights they then experience, some of them kill themselves by penances, and others weaken themselves by fasting. They take upon themselves more than they can bear, without rule or advice ; they try to conceal their austerities from those whom they are bound to obey, and some even venture to practise them though commanded to abstain.

There are also unreasonable people who undervalue submission and obedience, which is the penance of the reason and judgment, and therefore a more acceptable and sweet sacrifice unto God than all the acts of bodily penance.

And these beginners conduct themselves in the same way when they are praying ; they imagine that the whole business of prayer consists in sensible devotion, and this they strive to obtain with all their might, wearying out their brains and perplexing all the faculties of their souls. When they miss that sensible devotion, they are cast down, thinking they have done nothing. For this reason, it is most necessary that they should enter into the dark night that they may be cleansed from this childishness.

The perfection and value of things consist not in the multitude thereof, but in our knowing how to deny ourselves in them.

VI. ENVY AND SLOTH

Many are often vexed because of other men's goodness. They are sensibly afflicted when others outstrip them on the spiritual road, and will not endure to hear them praised. They become fretful over other men's virtues, and are sometimes unable to refrain from contradiction when they are commended ; they depreciate them as much as they can, looking on them with an evil eye.

As to spiritual sloth, beginners are wont to find their most spiritual occupations irksome, and avoid them as repugnant to their taste.

NEED FOR THE DARK NIGHT

In this night God weans beginners from the breasts of sweetness, in pure aridities and interior darkness, cleanses them from all imperfections and childish ways, and by ways most different makes them grow in virtue. For after all the exertions of beginners to mortify themselves in their actions and passions, their success will not be perfect, or even great, until God Himself shall do it for them in the purgation of the dark night.[1]

§ WHAT THE DARK NIGHT IS

By the dark night I mean contemplation. It produces in spiritual men two sorts of darkness or purgations conformable to the two divisions of man's nature into sensual and spiritual. Thus the first night, or sensual purgation, wherein the soul is purified or detached, will be of the senses, subjecting them to the spirit. The other is that night or spiritual purgation wherein the soul is purified and detached in the spirit, and which subdues and disposes it for union with God in love. The night of sense is common, and the lot of many : these are the beginners, of whom I shall first speak. The spiritual night is the portion of very few ; and they are those who have made some progress, exercised therein, of whom I shall speak hereafter.

I may pass on to treat more at large of spiritual night ; for of that very little has been said, either by word of mouth or in writing, and little is known of it even by experience.

[1] " Without contemplation one will never make much progress in virtue, and one will never be much use in helping the progress of others. One never will get quite free from one's weaknesses and imperfections. One will be always attached to earth, and one will never rise much above the feelings of nature. One will never be able to serve God with perfection. But with contemplation one will do more, both for oneself and for others, in a month, than one could do without it in ten years. It produces acts of excellence detached from the impurities of nature, very sublime acts of love of God such as can rarely be made without this gift ; and finally it perfects faith and all the other virtues, lifting them to the highest degree to which it is possible to rise."—P. LALLEMANT, S.J., *Doctrine Spirituelle : VIIe Principe*, Ch. IV.

RECOLLECTION IS FAVOURABLE TO THE DARK NIGHT

Recollected persons enter the dark night sooner than others, after they have begun their spiritual course; because they are kept at a greater distance from the occasions of falling away, and because they correct more quickly their worldly desires, which is necessary in order to begin to enter the blessed night of sense.

THREE SIGNS OF THE PASSIVE NIGHT OF THE SENSES

The first is this: when we find no comfort in the things of God, and none also in created things.

It is probable that this dryness is not the result of sins or of imperfections recently committed; for if it were, we should feel some inclination or desire for other things than those of God.

Inasmuch as this absence of pleasure in the things of heaven and of earth may proceed from bodily indisposition or a melancholy temperament, which frequently cause dissatisfaction with all things, the second test and condition become necessary.

The second test and condition of this purgation are that the memory dwells ordinarily upon God with a painful anxiety and carefulness, the soul thinks it is not serving God, but going backwards, because it is no longer conscious of any sweetness in the things of God. In that case it is clear that his weariness of spirit and aridity are not the results of weakness and lukewarmness; for the peculiarity of lukewarmness is the want of earnestness in, and of interior solicitude for, the things of God.

The cause of this dryness is that God is transferring to the spirit the goods and energies of the senses, which, being now unable to assimilate them, become dry, parched up, and empty; for the sensual nature of man is helpless in those things which belong to the spirit simply. Thus the spirit having tasted, the flesh shrinks and fails.

The substantial nature of its interior food, which is the commencement of contemplation, is dim and dry to the senses. This contemplation is in general secret, and unknown to him who is admitted into it, and with the aridity and emptiness which it produces in the senses, it makes the soul long for solitude and quiet, without the power of reflecting on anything distinctly, or even desiring to do so.

CONDUCT : PASSIVITY

Now, if they who are in this state knew how to be quiet, to disregard every interior and exterior work, —to be without solicitude about anything—they would have, in this tranquillity, a sense of their most delicate interior nourishment. This is so delicate that, in general, it eludes our perceptions if we make any special effort to feel it, for, as I am saying, it does its work when the soul is most tranquil and free; it is like the air which vanishes when we shut our hands to grasp it. If the soul will do anything in its own strength, it will hinder rather than aid God's work.

It was far otherwise once. The reason is this: God is now working in the soul, in the state of contemplation, that is, when it advances from meditation to the state of proficients, in such a way as to seem to have bound up all the interior faculties, leaving no help in the understanding, no sweetness in the will, no reflections in the memory. Therefore, at this time, all that the soul can do of itself ends, as I have said, in disturbing the peace and the work of God in the spirit amid the dryness of sense. This peace, being spiritual and delicate, effects a work that is quiet and delicate, unobtrusive and satisfactory, pacific and utterly alien from the former delights, which were perceptible and sensible.

The third sign we have for ascertaining whether this dryness be the purgation of sense, is inability to meditate and make reflections, and to excite the imagination, as before, notwithstanding all the efforts we may make ; for God begins now to communicate Himself, no longer through the channel of sense, as formerly, in consecutive reflections, by which we arranged and divided our knowledge, but in pure spirit, which admits not of successive reflections, and in the act of pure contemplation, to which neither the interior nor the exterior senses of our lower nature can ascend. Hence it is that the fancy and the imagination cannot help or suggest any reflections, nor use them ever afterwards.

As soon as we enter upon this state, the inability to make our meditations continually grows. It is true that this purgation at first is not continuous in some persons, for they are not altogether without sensible sweetness and comfort—their weakness renders their rapid weaning inexpedient—nevertheless, it grows upon them more and more, and the operations of sense diminish, if they are going on to perfection. They, however, who are not walking in the way of contemplation, meet with a very different treatment, for the night of aridities is not continuous with them, they are sometimes in it, and sometimes not; they are at one time unable to meditate, and at another able as before.

God leads these persons into this night only to try them and to humble them, and to correct their desires, that they may not grow up spiritual gluttons, and not for the purpose of leading them into the way of the spirit, which is contemplation. God does not raise to contemplation every one that is tried in the way of the spirit, nor even half of them, and He knoweth the reason. Hence it is that these persons are never wholly weaned from the breasts of meditations and reflections, but only, as I have said, at intervals and at certain seasons.

CONDUCT IN THE NIGHT OF THE SENSES
PASSAGE TO CONTEMPLATION

During the aridities of the night of sense—when God effects the change of which I have spoken, drawing the soul out of the way of sense into that of the spirit, from meditation to contemplation, where it is helpless in the things of God, so far as its own powers are concerned, spiritual persons have to endure great afflictions, not so much because of aridity, but because they are afraid that they will be lost on this road; thinking that they are spiritually ruined, and that God has forsaken them, because they find no help or consolation in holy things. Under these circumstances, they weary themselves, and strive, as they were wont, to fix the powers of the soul with some satisfaction upon some matter of meditation, imagining when they cannot do this, and are conscious of the effort, that they are doing nothing. This they do not without great dislike and inward unwillingness on the part of the soul, which enjoys its state of quietness and rest, the faculties not being at work.

In thus turning away from this state they make no progress in the other, because, by exerting their own spirit, they lose that spirit which they had, that of tranquillity and peace.

THE NEED OF A GOOD DIRECTOR

Under these circumstances, if they meet with no one who understands the matter, these persons fall away, and abandon the right road ; or become weak, or at least put hindrances in the way of their further advancement, because of the great efforts they make to proceed in their former way of meditation, fatiguing their natural powers beyond measure. They think that their state is the result of negligence or of sin.

MEDITATION SHOULD BE ABANDONED

The conduct to be observed in the night of sense is this : in nowise have recourse to meditations, for, as I have said, the time is now past, let the soul be quiet and at rest, though they may think they are doing nothing, that they are losing time, and that their lukewarmness is the reason of their unwillingness to employ their thoughts. They will do enough if they keep patience, and persevere in prayer ; all they have to do is to keep their soul free, unembarrassed, and at rest from all thoughts

and all knowledge, not anxious about their meditation,[1] contenting themselves simply with directing
their attention lovingly and calmly towards God;
and all this without anxiety or effort, or desire to
feel and taste His presence. For all such efforts
disquiet the soul, and distract it from the calm repose
and sweet tranquillity of contemplation to which
they are now admitted.

And though they may have many scruples that
they are wasting time, and that it may be better for
them to betake themselves to some other good work,
seeing that in prayer and meditation they are become
helpless; yet let them be patient with themselves,
and remain quiet, for that which they are uneasy
about is their own satisfaction and liberty of spirit.

When the soul interiorly rests, every action and
passion, or consideration at that time, will distract
and disturb it, and make it feel the dryness and
emptiness of sense. The more it strives to find
help in affections and knowledge, the more will it
feel the deficiency which cannot now be supplied in
that way. It is therefore expedient for the soul
which is in this condition not to be troubled because
its faculties have become useless, yea, rather it
should desire that they may become so quickly; for
by not hindering the operation of infused contemplation, to which God is now admitting it, the soul
is refreshed in peaceful abundance, and set on fire
with the spirit of love, which this contemplation,
dim and secret, induces and establishes within it.

[1] " As to God, we shall never attain to Him but by the complete
repose of the faculties of the intellect, no longer perceiving either
deification, nor life, nor substance which holds any exact comparison
with this primal cause, super-eminently raised above all things."—
DIONYSIUS: *Divine Names*, Chapter II.

FIRST IMPRESSIONS: ANXIOUS LOVE AND FEAR OF GOD

The burning fire of love, in general, is not felt at first, for it has not begun to burn, either because of our natural impurity, or because the soul, not understanding its own state, has not given it a peaceful rest within. Sometimes, however, whether it be so or not, a certain longing after God begins to be felt; and the more it grows, the more the soul feels itself touched and inflamed with the love of God, without knowing or understanding how or whence that love comes, except that at times this burning so inflames it that it longs earnestly after God.

This love, in general, is not felt at first, but only the dryness and emptiness of which I am speaking: and then, instead of love, which is afterwards enkindled, what the soul feels in the dryness and the emptiness of its faculties is a general painful anxiety about God, and a certain painful misgiving that it is not serving Him. But a soul anxious and afflicted for His sake is a sacrifice not a little pleasing unto God. Secret contemplation keeps the soul in this state of anxiety, until, in the course of time, having purged the sensual nature of man, in some degree, of its natural forces and affections by means of the aridities it occasions, it shall have kindled within it this divine love. But in the meantime, like a sick man in the hands of his physician, all it has to do, in the dark night and dry purgation of the desire, is to suffer, healing its many imperfections.

THE NARROW GATE

The narrow gate is this night of sense. The soul detaches itself from sense that it may enter on it, basing itself on faith, which is a stranger to all sense, that it may afterwards travel along the strait road of that other night—the night of the spirit, by which it advances towards God in most pure faith, which is the means of union with Him.

THE ADVANTAGES OF THE NIGHT OF THE SENSES

The spirit, being emptied and dried of all sensible sweetness, is given the bread of infused contemplation.

Of these, the first is the knowledge of self and its own vileness. By contrasting the abundance of satisfaction in former times and by the difficulty which good works now present to it, the soul is brought to a knowledge of its own vileness and misery, which in the season of prosperity it saw not.

It possesses and retains that excellent and necessary virtue of self-knowledge, counting itself for nothing, and having no satisfaction in itself, because it sees that of itself it does and can do nothing.

The soul learns to commune with God with more respect and reverence. . . . We learn how reverently and discreetly in spiritual detachment we are to converse with God. When the desires are quelled, and sensible joy and consolation withdrawn, the understanding remains free and clear for the reception of the truth.

" In a desert land, and inaccessible, and without

water ; so in the holy have I appeared to Thee, that I might see Thy strength and Thy glory." The Psalmist does not say here—and it is worthy of observation—that his previous sweetness and delight were any dispositions or means whereby he might come to the knowledge of the glory of God, but rather that it was through an aridity and emptying of the powers of sense, spoken of here as the barren and dry land.

Moreover, he does not say that his reflections and meditations on divine things, with which he was once familiar, had led him to the knowledge and contemplation of God's power, but, rather, his inability to meditate on God, to form reflections by the help of his imagination ; that is the inaccessible land.

SPIRITUAL HUMILITY

The soul, seeing itself parched and miserable, does not, even for a moment, think itself better than others. Out of this grows the love of our neighbour. . . . The soul sees nothing but its own misery, which it keeps so constantly before its eyes that it can look upon nothing else.

In this state, too, men are submissive and obedient in the spiritual way, for when they see their own wretchedness they not only listen to instruction, but desire to have it from anyone who will guide their steps and tell them what they ought to do.

MOMENTS OF ILLUMINATION

Sometimes, and even quite often, in the midst of aridities and hardship, God communicates to the soul, when it least expects it, spiritual sweetness, most pure love, and spiritual knowledge of the most exalted kind, of greater worth and profit than any of which it had previous experience, though at first the soul may not think so, for the spiritual influence now communicated is most delicate, and imperceptible by sense.

THAT WHICH DOMINATES

The fear of God and the desire to please Him increase in this arid night.

When the house of sensuality is at rest, that is, when the passions are mortified and concupiscence is quenched, the soul begins to set out on the way of the spirit, the way of those who progress and of proficients, which is also called the illuminative way.

THE DEVIL

Progress towards the night of the spirit is attended with heavy trials and temptations of sense of long continuance, in some longer than in others; for to some is sent the angel of Satan, the spirit of impurity, to buffet them with horrible and violent temptations of the flesh, to trouble their minds with filthy thoughts, and their imaginations with representations of sin most vividly depicted; which, at times, becomes an affliction more grievous than death.

At other times this night is attended by the spirit of blasphemy; the thoughts and conceptions are overrun with intolerable blasphemies, which now and then are suggested to the imagination with such violence as almost to break forth in words; this, too, is a heavy affliction.

Again, another hateful spirit, called by the prophet " the spirit of giddiness," is suffered to torment them. This spirit so clouds their judgment that they are filled with a thousand scruples and perplexities so embarrassing that they can never satisfy themselves about them, nor submit their judgment therein to the counsel and direction of others.

DURATION OF THE PURIFICATION

These trials are measured by the divine will, and are proportioned to the imperfections, many or few, to be purged away : and also to the degree of union in love to which God intends to raise the soul : that is the measure of its humiliations, both in their intensity and duration.

Those who are strong and more able to bear suffering, are purified in more intense trials, and in less time. But those who are weak are purified very slowly, with weak temptations, and the night of their purgation is long : their senses are refreshed from time to time lest they should fall away ; these, however, come late to the pureness of their perfection in this life, and some of them never. These persons are not clearly in the purgative night, nor clearly out of it ; for though they make no progress, yet in order that they may be humble and know themselves, God tries them for a season in aridities and temptations, and visits them with His consolations at intervals lest they should become faint-hearted, and seek for comfort in the ways of the world.

BOOK II

THE PASSIVE NIGHT OF THE SPIRIT

THE passive night of the spirit is exceptional in its complete manifestation and its terrible torments are compensated by wonderful graces. This purification alone disposes the soul to the highest union with God.

THE TRANSITION BETWEEN THE TWO NIGHTS

The soul, which God is leading onwards, enters not into the night of the spirit at once when it has passed through the aridities and trials of the first purgation and night of sense ; yea, rather it must spend some time, perhaps years, after quitting the state of beginners, in exercising itself in the state of proficients.

In this state—as one released from a rigorous imprisonment—it occupies itself in divine things with much greater freedom and satisfaction, and its joy is more abundant and interior than it was in the beginning before it entered the night of sense ; its imagination and faculties are not held, as hitherto, in the bonds of meditation and spiritual reflections ; it now rises at once to most tranquil and loving contemplation, and finds spiritual sweetness without the fatigue of meditation.

It is in this way that God purifies some souls who are not to rise to so high a degree of love as others. He admits them at intervals into the night of contemplation or spiritual purgation, causing the sun to shine upon them, and then to hide its face, according to the words of the Psalmist: " He sendeth His crystal," that is contemplation, " like morsels." These morsels of dim contemplation are, however, never so intense as is that awful night of contemplation of which I am speaking, and in which God purposely places the soul, that He may raise it to the divine union.

PHYSICAL EFFECTS——ECSTASIES

But as the sensual part of the soul is weak, without any capacity for the strong things of the spirit, they who are in the state of proficients by reason of the spiritual communications made to the sensual part, are subject therein to great infirmities and sufferings, and physical derangements, and consequently weariness of mind. Hence the communications made to these cannot be very strong, intense, or spiritual, such as they are required to be for the divine union with God, because of the weakness and corruption of the sensual part which has a share in them.

Here is the source of ecstasies, raptures, and dislocation of the bones which always happen whenever these communications are not purely spiritual ; that is, granted to the mind alone, as in the case of the perfect, already purified in the second night of the spirit. In these, raptures and physical sufferings have no place, for they enjoy liberty of spirit with unclouded and unsuspended senses.

IMPERFECTIONS OF PROFICIENTS

They suffer from dullness of mind, and natural rudeness which every man contracts by sin ; from distraction and dissipation of mind, which must be refined, enlightened, and made recollected in the sufferings and hardships of this night.

The devil causes many both to believe in vain visions and false prophecies, and to presume that God and His saints are speaking to them : they also frequently believe in their own fancies.

Satan, too, is wont to fill them with pride and presumption ; and they, led on by vanity and arrogance, make a show of themselves in the performance of exterior acts which have an air of sanctity, such as ecstasies and other appearances. They thus become bold with God, losing holy fear, which is the key and guard of all virtue. Some of them become so entangled in manifold falsehoods and delusions, and so persist in them, that their return to the pure road of virtue and real spirituality is exceedingly doubtful. They fall into this miserable condition because they gave way to these spiritual imaginations and feelings with overmuch confidence when they began to advance on the road of spirituality.

HOW GOD DESPOILS THE OLD MAN

God now denudes the faculties, the affections, and feelings, spiritual and sensual, interior and exterior, leaving the understanding in darkness, the will dry, the memory empty, the affections of the soul in the deepest affliction, bitterness, and distress[1] ; withholding from it the former sweetness it had in spiritual things, in order that this privation may be one of the principles, of which the mind has need, that the spiritual form of the spirit, which is the union of love, may enter into it and be one with it. . . . All this our Lord effects in the soul by means of contemplation, pure and dark.

CONTEMPLATION IN DARKNESS

The dark night is a certain inflowing of God into the soul which cleanses it of its ignorances and imperfections, habitual, natural, and spiritual. Contemplatives call it infused contemplation, or mystical theology, whereby God secretly teaches the soul and instructs it in the perfection of love, without efforts on its own part beyond a loving attention to God, listening to His voice and admitting the light He sends, but without understanding how this is infused contemplation. And inasmuch as it is the loving wisdom of God, it produces special effects in the soul, for it prepares it, by purifying and enlightening it, for union with God in love : it is the same loving wisdom, which by enlightening purifies the blessed spirits, that here purifies and enlightens the soul.

The divine wisdom is, for two reasons, not night and darkness only, but pain and torment also to the soul. The first is, the divine wisdom is so high

[1] " Once, the intelligence, the memory and the will felt Your love in everything that happened in them. . . . Now, on the contrary, I am naked and despoiled of everything, and I find myself unable to love and hope as before. What then can I do, being at once alive and dead, and deprived of the intelligence, the memory and the will, and, what is still worse, of love ? "—St. CATHERINE OF GENOA: *Dialogues II*, Chapter II.

that it transcends the capacity of the soul, and therefore is, in that respect, darkness. The second reason is based on the meanness and impurity of the soul, and in that respect the divine wisdom is painful to it, afflictive and dark also.

DARKNESS

Mystic theologians call infused contemplation a ray of darkness, that is, for the unenlightened and unpurified soul, because this great supernatural light masters the natural power of the reason and takes away its natural way of understanding.

SUFFERINGS

Because the light and wisdom of contemplation is most pure and bright, and because the soul, on which it beats, is in darkness and impure, that soul which is the recipient must greatly suffer.

And when the rays of this pure light strike upon the soul, in order to expel its impurities, the soul perceives itself to be so unclean and miserable that it seems as if God had set Himself against it, and itself were set against God.

This is the fruit of that deep impression, made on the mind, in the knowledge and sense of its own wickedness and misery. For now the divine and dim light reveals to it all its wretchedness, and it sees clearly that of itself it can never be other than it is.

For when this divine contemplation strikes it with a certain vehemence, in order to strengthen it and subdue it, it is then so pained in its weakness as almost to faint away particularly at times when the divine contemplation strikes it with greater vehemence; for sense and spirit, as if under a heavy and gloomy burden, suffer and groan in agony so great that death itself would be a desired relief.

The soul under the burden of this oppression feels itself so removed out of God's favour that it thinks—and so it is—that all things which consoled it formerly have utterly failed it, and that no one is left to pity it.

The divine touches the soul to renew it and to ripen it, in order to make it divine, to detach it from the habitual affections and qualities of the old man, to which it clings and conforms itself. The divine extreme so breaks and bruises the spiritual substance, swallowing it up in profound darkness, that the soul, at the sight of its own wretchedness, seems to perish and waste away, by a cruel spiritual death, as if it were swallowed up and devoured by a wild beast, suffering the pangs of Jonah in the belly of the whale.

But the greatest affliction of the sorrowful soul in this state is the thought that God has abandoned it, of which it has no doubt; that He has cast it away into darkness as an abominable thing.

It has also the same sense of abandonment with respect to all creatures, and that it is an object of contempt to all, especially to its friends.[1]

---

[1] " Blinded by self-love we cling excessively to all that seems to us beautiful, good and just, and we love it as such. But Pure Love, seeing us so disposed, destroys and dispenses one after the other the things to which we are attached, through death, sickness, poverty, hatred, scandal and discord. It strikes us through our parents, our friends, ourselves; we do not know what to do with ourselves; torn from the things that delight us we receive from

The soul is conscious of a profound emptiness, and destitution of the three kinds of goods, natural, temporal, and spiritual. The sensual part is purified in aridities, the faculties in the emptiness of their powers, and the spirit in the thick darkness.

All this God brings about by means of this dim contemplation, in which the soul is made to suffer from the failure and withdrawal of its natural powers, which is a most distressing pain. It is like that of a person being suffocated, or hindered from breathing. But this contemplation is also purifying the soul, undoing or emptying it, or consuming in it, as fire consumes the rust and mouldiness of metal, all the affections and habits of imperfection which it had contracted in the whole course of its life.

They are occasionally felt so acutely that the soul seems literally to suffer the pains of hell . . . and to have its purgatory in this life ; for this is the purgation which would have been endured there. Thus the soul which passes through this state in the present life, either enters not into purgatory, or is detained there but a moment, for one hour here is of greater profit than many there.

The afflictions and distress of the will now are also very great ; they occasionally pierce the soul with a sudden recollection of the evils that environ it, and of the uncertainty of relief. To this is superadded the memory of past happiness ; for they who enter this night have, generally, had much sweetness in

---

them nothing but pain and confusion. . . . When the Divine Love has held us thus for a time, with our souls suspended, almost despairing, bored and disgusted with all that they loved before, He shows Himself to us, with His heavenly face all joyous and resplendent."— ST. CATHERINE OF GENOA : *Life*, by the Bollandists.

God, and served Him greatly ; but now, to see themselves strangers to so much happiness, and unable
to recover it, causes them the greatest affliction.

The soul derives no consolation now in the advice
that may be given it, or from its spiritual director,
because of the loneliness and desolation of this dark
night. Though its confessor may set before it in
many ways good reasons why it should be com-
forted because of the blessings which these pains
supply, the soul will not believe him. For as it is
so filled with and overwhelmed by its sense of these
evils, whereby it discerns so clearly its own misery,
it imagines that its spiritual director, not seeing that
which itself sees and feels, speaks as he does without
comprehending its state.

The soul must wait until it is softened, humbled,
and purified ; until it becomes so refined, simple,
and pure, as to become one with the Spirit of God
in that degree of the union of love which He in His
mercy intends for it, and corresponding to which is
the greater or less violence, the longer or shorter
duration, of this purgation.

But if this purgation is to be real it will last, notwithstanding its vehemence, for some years, but
admitting of intermissions and relief, during which,
by the dispensation of God, the dim contemplation
divested of its purgative form and character assumes
that of the illuminative and of love.

As the dark night hinders the exercise of the
faculties and affections, it cannot lift up the heart
and mind to God as before, nor pray to Him. . . .
If at any time it prays, it prays with so much aridity,

and without sweetness, so as to think that God neither hears nor regards it. . . . And, in truth, this is not the time for the soul to speak to God, but . . . to put its " mouth in the dust," suffering in patience this purgation.

It is God Himself Who is now working in the soul, and the soul is therefore powerless. Hence it comes that it cannot pray or give much attention to divine things. Neither can it attend to temporal matters, for it falls into frequent distractions, and the memory is so profoundly weakened, that many hours pass by without its knowing what it has done or thought, what it is doing or is about to do ; nor can it give much heed to what it is occupied with, notwithstanding all its efforts.

These wanderings and failures of the memory are the result of interior recollection, by which the soul is absorbed in contemplation. For in order to prepare the soul, and temper it divinely in all its powers for the divine union of love, it must, first of all, be absorbed with all its powers in the divine and dim spiritual light of contemplation, and be thus detached from all affection for, and apprehension of, created things. This continues ordinarily in proportion to the intensity of its contemplation. Thus, the more pure and simple the divine light when it beats on the soul, the more does it darken it, empty it, and annihilate it, as to all its apprehensions and affections, whether they regard heavenly or earthly things. And also, the less pure and simple the light, the less is the soul darkened and annihilated.

The spiritual light falling on the soul if there is anything to reflect it, that is, upon any matter, however small, of perfection, which presents itself to the understanding or a decision to be made as to the truth or falsehood of anything, the soul sees it at once, and understands the matter more clearly than it ever did before it entered into this darkness. In the same way the soul discerns the spiritual light which is given it that it may easily recognise its own imperfection. . . .

Then, because this spiritual light is so clear, pure, and diffused, neither confined to, nor specially related to, any particular matter of the understanding, natural or divine, seeing that with respect to all such matters the powers of the soul are empty and as if they did not exist—the soul in great ease and freedom discerns and searches into everything high or low, that is presented to it; and for that reason the Apostle said, "The Spirit searcheth all things, even the profundities of God;"[1] for it is of this pure and diffused wisdom that we are to understand that which the Holy Ghost spake by the mouth of the wise man, "Wisdom reacheth everywhere by reason of her clearness;" that is, because not connected with any particular object of the understanding or affection. The characteristic of a mind purified and annihilated as to all particular objects of affection and of the understanding, is to have no pleasure in, or knowledge of, anything in particular; to abide in emptiness and darkness; to embrace all things in its grand comprehensiveness, that it may fulfil mystically the words of the Apostle, "having nothing and possessing all things."[2]

[1] 2 Cor. vi. 10.
[2] "It is our ambition to enter into this luminous darkness and to see and know, precisely by the effect of our blindness and our mystical ignorance, Him who escapes all contemplation and all knowledge."—DIONYSIUS : *Myst. Theol.*, Chapter II.

THE EFFECTS OF THE PASSIVE NIGHT OF THE SPIRIT

Without this purgation it is altogether impossible to taste of the abundance of these spiritual delights. For one single affection remaining in the soul, or any one matter to which the mind clings either habitually or actually, is sufficient to prevent all perception and all communication of the tender and interior sweetness of the spirit of love. . . . So the mind which is still subject to any actual or habitual affection or particular or narrow mode of apprehending, or understanding anything, cannot taste the sweetness of the spirit of liberty, according to the desire of the will.[1]

This darkness must continue so long as it is necessary to destroy the habit, long ago contracted, of understanding things in a natural way, and until the divine enlightening shall have taken its place. For this night is drawing the spirit away from its ordinary and common sense of things, that it may draw it towards the divine sense, which is a stranger and an alien to all human ways ; so much so that the soul seems to be carried out of itself. At other times it looks upon itself as if under the influence of some charm or spell, and is amazed at all that it hears and sees, which seem to it to be most strange and out of the way, though in reality they are, as they usually are, the same as what formerly occupied it.

[1] " And, we dare to deny everything about God in order to penetrate into this sublime ignorance, which is veiled from us by all that we know of other beings, and to contemplate this supernatural darkness which is hidden from our view by that which we find luminous in other beings."—DIONYSIUS, *Myst. Theol.*, Chapter II.

THE SOUL BEGINS TO BURN IN THE DARKNESS

There is a certain fire of love in the spirit whereby the soul, amidst these dark trials, feels itself wounded to the quick by this strong love divine with a certain sense and foretaste of God, though it understands nothing distinctly, because the understanding is in darkness.

The spirit is now conscious of deep love, for this spiritual burning produces the passion of it.

In all its works and thoughts, in all its employments and on every occasion, the soul loves and longs in many ways, and this longing also is manifold in its forms, always and everywhere present; the soul has no rest.

The soul, however, amidst these gloomy and loving pains, is conscious of a certain companionship and inward strength which attends upon it and so invigorates it that if the burden of this oppressive darkness be removed, it oftentimes feels itself desolate, empty, and weak. The reason is that the force and courage communicated to the soul flow passively from the dark fire of love which assails it, and so, when that fire ceases to assail it, the darkness, the strength, and fire of love at the same time cease in the soul.

LOVE OR KNOWLEDGE

As these spiritual treasures are passively infused into the soul by God, the will indeed may love and yet the understanding not understand, and likewise the understanding may be active while the will remains without love; for as the dark night of contemplation comprises both divine light and love, just as fire has light and heat, it is not surprising that this loving light sometimes striking the will enkindles in it love, the understanding meanwhile remaining in darkness because the light has not fallen on it; at other times the light striking the understanding enlightens it and bestows knowledge on it while leaving the will dry, just as one might perceive the heat of fire without seeing its light, or the light without feeling any warmth, for it is the Lord who acts thus, infusing His gifts as He likes.

THE UNDERSTANDING MUST BE PURIFIED

Sometimes the understanding and the will unite themselves: the more the understanding is purified the more perfect and delicate, at times, is the union of the understanding and the will. But, before the soul attains to this state, it is more common for the touch of the fire of love to be felt in the will than for the touch of the perfect intelligence to be felt in the understanding.

On the other hand, the receptive passion of the understanding can only receive knowledge purely and passively—and this only when it has been purified—therefore previous to purgation the soul feels less frequently the touch of knowledge than the passion of love, for this latter does not require that the soul should be so thoroughly purified concerning its passions, since these precisely help it in feeling passionate love.

It may be observed here that, although at first, in the beginning of the spiritual night, this burning love is not felt because the fire of love has not yet done its work, God communicates to the soul, instead of it, a reverent love of Himself so great that the heaviest trials and deepest afflictions of this night are the distressing thought that it has lost God, and that He has abandoned it. It may, therefore, be always said that from the beginning of this night the soul is full of the anxieties of love, at one time that of reverence, at another that of burning. It is evident that the greatest of its sufferings is this doubt.

But when the fire of love and the reverent love of God together have set the soul in a flame, it is wont to gain such strength and energy, and such eager longing after God—effects of this glowing love— that it boldly disregards all considerations, and sets everything aside, in the inebriating force of love, and, without much consideration of its acts, it conducts itself strangely and extravagantly in every way that it may come to Him whom the soul loveth.

This is the reason why Mary Magdalene, though so noble, heeded not the many guests, high and low, who were feasting, as we read in St. Luke, in the house of the Pharisee.

WHY THE LIGHT BRINGS DARKNESS AND SUFFERING

I must not omit here to say why it is that the divine light, although always light to the soul, does not illumine it the moment it strikes it, as it does at a later time, but brings with it only darkness and misery. . . . The divine light gives light at once, but the soul sees nothing at first but that which is immediately before it, or rather within itself; its own darkness and misery. . . . Later, when it has been purified by the knowledge and sense of its misery, it will have eyes to discern the blessings of the divine light, and being delivered and set free from all darkness and imperfections, the great blessings and profit will become known which the soul is gaining for itself in this blessed night.

SUMMARY

By correcting and drying up all affections of sense and spirit, by weakening and wasting the natural attachment of the soul to inferior things, God makes the soul die to all that is not God, that, being denuded and stripped, it may clothe itself anew. This is nothing else but the supernatural light giving light to the understanding, so that the human understanding becomes divine, made one with the divine.

THE DESIRES ARE CALLED

The desires of sense and spirit are lulled to sleep and mortified, unable to relish anything either human or divine; the affections of the soul are thwarted and brought low, become helpless and have nothing to rest upon; the imagination is fettered, and unable to make any profitable reflections, the memory is gone, and the will, too, is dry and afflicted, and all the faculties are empty and useless, and, moreover, a dense and heavy cloud over-shadows the soul, distresses it and holds it as if it were far away from God.

THE SECURITY OF THIS STATE OF DARKNESS

The reason of this safety has been clearly shown : for usually the soul never errs, except under the influence of its desires, or tastes, or reflections, or understanding, or affections. . . . It is therefore clear that the soul is secure against being led astray by them, when all these operations and movements have ceased. Because then the soul is delivered, not only from itself, but also from its other enemies—the world and the devil—who, when the affections and operations of the soul have ceased, cannot assault it by any other way or by any other means.

It follows from this, that the greater the darkness and emptiness of its natural operations in which the soul travels, the greater is its security.

The interior acts and movements of the soul, if they are to be divinely influenced by God, must be first of all lulled to sleep, darkened and subdued, in their natural state, so far as their capacity and operations are concerned, until they lose all their strength.

O spiritual soul, when thou seest thy desire obscured, thy will arid and constrained, and thy faculties incapable of any interior act, be not grieved at this, but look upon it rather as a great good, for God is delivering thee from thyself, taking the matter out of thy hands.

THE SOUL MAKES PROGRESS IN THE DARKNESS

The soul makes greater progress when it least thinks so, yea, most frequently when it imagines that it is losing.

The soul makes the greater progress when it travels in the dark, not knowing the way.

There is another reason also why the soul has travelled safely in this obscurity; it has suffered: for the way of suffering is safer, and also more profitable, than that of rejoicing and of action. In suffering God gives strength, but in action and in joy the soul does but show its own weakness and imperfections.

The truth is, that the nearer the soul comes to Him it perceives that darkness is greater and deeper because of its own weakness; thus the nearer the sun the greater the darkness and distress wrought by its great brightness, because our eyes are weak, imperfect, and defective. Hence it is that the spiritual light of God is so immeasurable, so far above the understanding, that when it comes near to it, it dims and blinds it.

If a man wishes to be sure of the road he travels on, he must close his eyes and walk in the dark.

THIS DARK CONTEMPLATION IS SECRET

First, this dark contemplation is called secret, because it is the mystical theology which theologians call secret wisdom, and which, according to St. Thomas, is infused into the soul more especially by love. This happens in a secret hidden way in which the natural operations of the understanding and the other faculties have no share. And, therefore, because the faculties of the soul cannot compass it, it being the Holy Ghost Who infuses it into the soul, in a way it knoweth not, as the Bride saith in the Canticle, we call it secret.[1]

And, in truth, it is not the soul only that knows it not, but no one else, not even the devil.

It is secret also in its effects. It is not only secret beyond the powers of the soul to speak of it, during the darkness and sharpness of the purgation, when the secret wisdom is purifying the soul, but afterwards also, during· the illumination, when that wisdom is most clearly communicated, it is so secret that it cannot be discerned or described. Moreover, the soul has no wish to speak of it, and besides, it can discover no way or proper similitude to describe it by, so as to make known a knowledge so high, a spiritual impression so delicate and infused. Yea and if it could have a wish to speak of it, and find terms to describe it, it would always remain secret still.

This interior wisdom is so simple, general, and spiritual, that it enters not into the understanding under any form or image subject to sense, as is sometimes the case, the imagination, therefore, and the

---

[1] " I wish you never to concern yourself with what I am doing, for you would always rob something of it in appropriating to yourself that which does not belong to you. I shall therefore carry out the rest of my work without your knowing anything about it : I wish to separate you from your spirit so that it should seem drowned in my depths.

" God works in us as He wishes, so subtly and secretly that the man in whom the work is being accomplished does not himself perceive it. . . . And if that man knew of the work he would always spoil it."—St. CATHERINE OF GENOA : *Dialogues*, ii., Chapter II.

senses—as it has not entered in by them, nor is modified by them—cannot account for it, nor form any conception of it, so as to speak in any degree correctly about it, though the soul be distinctly conscious that it feels and tastes this sweet and strange wisdom.

This explains why some persons, walking in this way, good and timid souls, who, when they would give an account of their interior state to their directors, know not how to do it, neither have they the power to do it, and so feel a great repugnance to explain themselves, especially when contemplation is the more simple and with difficulty discernible by them. All they can say is that their soul is satisfied, calm, or contented, that they have a sense of the presence of God, and that all goes well with them, as they think; but they cannot explain their state, except by general expressions of this kind. But it is a different matter when they have a consciousness of particular things, such as visions, impressions, and the like.

Mystical wisdom has the property of hiding the soul within itself. For beside its ordinary operation, it sometimes so absorbs the soul and plunges it in this secret abyss that the soul sees itself distinctly as far away from, and abandoned by, all created things; it looks upon itself as one that is placed in a wild and vast solitude whither no human being can come, as in an immense wilderness without limits; a wilderness, the more delicious, sweet, and lovely, the more it is wide, vast, and lonely, where the soul is the more hidden, the more it is raised up above all created things. It not only understands how mean are all created things in relation to the supreme

wisdom and divine knowledge, but also, how low
defective, and, in a certain sense, improper, are a
the words and phrases by which in this life w
discuss divine things, and how utterly impossibl
it is by any natural means, however profoundl
and learnedly we may speak, to understand and se
them as they are, except in the light of mystica
theology.

THE TEN DEGREES OF THE MYSTICAL LADDER O DIVINE LOVE

The first degree of love makes the soul languisl
to its great profit. . . .   As a sick man loses th
desire for, and the taste of all food . . . so the sou
in this degree of love loses all pleasure in earthl
things, and all desire of them, and changes its colou1
that is, the conditions of the past life. It finds n
comfort, pleasure, nor support anywhere.

So anxious is the soul now that it seeks th
Beloved in all things ; all its thoughts, words, an
works are referred to Him ; in eating, sleeping, an
waking, all its anxieties are about Him.

The third step of the ladder of love renders th
soul active and fervent, so that it faints not. Th
soul, because of the great love it has for God, is i1
great pain and suffering because of the scantiness o
its service. . . .   It looks upon itself therefore a
unprofitable in all it does, and on its life as worthless
Another most wonderful effect is that it looks upo1
itself as being in truth the very worst of all souls
On this third step the soul is very far from givin;

way to vainglory or presumption, or from condemning others.

When the soul is on the fourth step of the ladder of love, it falls into a state of suffering, but without weariness. . . . It seeks not for consolation or sweetness either in God or elsewhere, neither does it pray for God's gifts, seeing clearly how many it has already received. For all it cares for now is how it shall please God, and serve Him in some measure in return for His goodness, and for the graces it has received, and this at any and every cost. This degree of love is exceedingly high.

On the fifth step of the ladder the soul longs after God, and desires Him with impatience. Great is the eagerness of the soul on this step to embrace, and be united to, the Beloved.

When the soul has ascended to the sixth step, it runs swiftly to God from Whom it receives many touches ; and hope too runs without fainting, for love that has made it strong makes it fly rapidly.

On the seventh step the soul becomes vehemently bold, in this intense and loving exaltation, no prudence can withhold it, no counsel control it, no shame restrain it ; for the favour which God hath shown it has made it vehemently bold.

On the eighth step the soul embraces the Beloved and holds Him fast. . . . On this step of union the desires of the soul are satisfied, but not without interruption. Some souls ascend to this step and at once fall back ; if they did not, and remained there, they would have attained to a certain state of blessedness in this life, and thus the soul tarries but briefly on this step of the ladder.

On the ninth step the soul is on fire sweetly. This step is that of the perfect who burn away sweetly in God, for this sweet and delicious burning is the work of the Holy Ghost because of the union of the soul with God. St. Gregory says of the Apostles, that they burned interiorly with love sweetly, when the Holy Ghost descended upon them.

On the tenth step of the ladder the soul becomes wholly assimilated unto God in the beatific vision which it then immediately enjoys; for having ascended in this life to the ninth, it goeth forth out of the body. For these—they are few—being perfectly purified by love, do not pass through purgatory.

THE DARKNESS PROTECTS FROM THE DEVIL

The more spiritual the communication is, and the further it is removed beyond the reach of sense, the less able is the devil to perceive it. This being so, it greatly concerns the soul's security, that the lower senses should be in the dark, and have no knowledge of the interior conversation of the soul with God.

ATTACKS OF THE DEVIL

It is very true, that oftentimes when these interior and most secret spiritual communications are made to the soul, the devil, though he knows neither their nature nor their form, ascertains their presence, and that the soul is then receiving some great blessings, merely from observing the silence and repose some of them effect in the senses, and in the powers of our lower nature. And then, when he sees that he cannot thwart them in the inmost depth of the soul, he does all he can to disquiet and disturb the sensual part which is accessible to him, now by pain and at another time by horrible dread, intending thereby to trouble the higher and spiritual part of the soul, and to frustrate the blessings it then receives and enjoys.

But very often when this contemplation pours its light purely into the spirit and exerts its strength therein, the devil, with all his efforts, is not able to disturb it, for then the soul becomes the recipient of renewed benefits, love, and a more secure peace; for, wonderful to tell! in its consciousness of the disturbing presence of the foe, it enters deeply into itself, without knowing how it comes to pass and without any action on its own part, and feels assured of a certain refuge where it can hide itself beyond the reach of the evil one; and thus its peace and joy are increased, of which the devil attempted to rob it.

At other times, when the spiritual communications flow over into the senses, the devil succeeds the more easily in disquieting the mind, and in disturbing it with the terrors with which he assails it through the senses.

This attack of the devil takes place also when God bestows His favours upon a soul by the instrumentality of a good angel; sometimes he even perceives the favours granted by God Himself, and ordinarily those bestowed on the soul through the instrumentality of a good angel become known to the enemy, that he may do what he can, according to the measure of justice, against that soul, and that he may be debarred from pleading that he had no opportunity of seizing on that soul.

When such a soul has real visions, through the instrumentality of an angel (this being the rule, whereas it hardly ever happens that Christ appears in His own person), God suffers the evil spirit to represent false visions of the same kind, in such a way that an incautious soul may be very easily deluded.

Sometimes, too, the evil spirit prevails and infests the soul with this horror and trouble, and this is a greater torment to the soul than all the evils of this life can be; for this horrible communication goes straight from spirit to spirit, divested of all that is corporal, in a manner painful beyond all bodily suffering. All this passes in the soul without its doing or undoing anything of itself to bring about these representations or impressions. . . . According to the measure of the dark purgation it has undergone, the soul enters on the fruition of sweet spiritual contemplation, and that so sublime at times that no language can describe it. It is the horror of the evil spirit which so refines the soul as to render it capable of this great good.

SUBSTANTIAL TOUCHES
THE HIGHEST DEGREE OF PRAYER

God, being the sovereign Lord, dwells substantially in the soul, and neither angel nor devil can discover what is going on there, nor penetrate the profound and secret communications which take place between Him and the soul. These communications, because the work of our Lord Himself, are wholly divine and supreme, and, as it were, substantial touches of the divine union between Himself and the soul; in one of these, because it is the highest possible degree of prayer, the soul receives greater good than in all the rest. Then indeed the evil spirit would not venture to assail the soul, because he could not succeed, neither can he know of those divine touches in the substance of the soul with the loving substance of God. No man can arrive at this blessed condition but by the most perfect purgation and detachment, by being spiritually hidden from all created things.

Darkness has deprived it of all things—yet love and faith, now burning within it, drawing the heart towards the Beloved, influence and guide it, and make it fly upwards to God along the road of solitude, while it knows neither how nor by what means that is done.

THE LIVING FLAME OF LOVE

O Living Flame of Love,
That woundest tenderly
My soul in its inmost depth!
As thou art no longer grievous,
Perfect thy work, if it be thy will,
Break the web of this sweet encounter.

O sweet burn!
O delicious wound!
O tender hand! O gentle touch!
Savouring of everlasting life,
And paying the whole debt,
By slaying Thou hast changed death into life.

O lamps of fire,
In the splendours of which
The deep caverns of sense,
Dim and dark,
With unwonted brightness
Give light and warmth together to their Beloved!

How gently and how lovingly
Thou wakest in my bosom,
Where alone Thou secretly dwellest;
And in Thy sweet breathing
Full of grace and glory,
How tenderly Thou fillest me with Thy love.

PROLOGUE

THE stanzas of the Living Flame speak of a love still more perfect and complete.

The soul already transformed, and glowing interiorly in the fire of love, is not only united with the divine fire, but becomes a living flame.

The action of the Holy Ghost within it is to kindle it and set it on fire; this is the burning of love, in union with which the will loves most deeply, being now one by love with that flame of fire. And thus the soul's acts of love are most precious, and even one of them more meritorious than many elicited not in the state of transformation.

Hence then we may say of the soul which is transformed in love, that its ordinary state is that of the fuel in the midst of the fire; that the acts of such a soul are the flames which rise up out of the fire of love.

And as the soul, in its present condition, cannot elicit acts without a special inspiration of the Holy Ghost, all its acts must be divine . . . its acts are divine in God.

The Holy Ghost is aflame in the soul. . . . God Himself is the author of this joy of the soul and spirit; the soul doeth nothing of itself. Inasmuch as the soul cannot work naturally here, nor make any efforts of its own otherwise then through the bodily senses and by their help—of which it is in this case completely free, and from which it is most detached —the work of the soul is solely to receive what God communicates, Who alone in the depths of the soul, without the help of the senses, can influence and direct it, and operate within it. Thus, then, all the movements of such a soul are divine, and though of God, still they are the soul's, because God effects them within it, itself willing them and assenting to them.

THE PURGATIVE WAY

PURIFICATION BY FIRE

The fire penetrates the substance of the fuel, playing about it, stripping it of its ugliness; the fuel is made ready to be all afire itself and to be transformed into fire. And all this is called in spiritual language the purgative way.

The soul suffers greatly in this spiritual exercise, and endures grievous afflictions of spirit which occasionally overflow into the senses; then the flame is felt to be grievous, for in this state of purgation the flame does not burn brightly, but is darksome, and if it gives forth any light at all it is only to show to the soul and make it feel all its miseries and defects; neither is it sweet, but painful, and if it kindles a fire of love that fire causes torments and uneasiness; it does not bring delight, but aridity, for although God in His kindness may send the soul some comfort to strengthen and animate it He makes it pay, both before and after, with sufferings and trials. It is not a refreshing and peaceful fire, but a consuming and searching one that makes the soul faint away and grieve at the sight of Self; not a glorious brightness, for it embitters the soul and makes it miserable, owing to the spiritual light it throws on Self.

At this juncture, the soul suffers in the understanding from deep darkness, in the will from aridity and conflict, and in the memory from the consciousness of its miseries. The eye of the spiritual understanding is clear, and in its very substance the soul suffers from poverty and dereliction. Dry and cold, yea, at times, even hot though it be, nothing gives the soul relief, nor has it a single good thought to console it and to help it to lift up the heart to God.

Suffering all these things together, the soul undergoes, as it were, its Purgatory, for all happiness being taken away the torture is hardly inferior to the torments of Purgatory.

The virtues and properties of God, being in the highest degree perfect, arise and make war within the soul, on the habits and properties of man which are in the highest degree imperfect. For since this flame gives forth a dazzling light it penetrates the darkness of the soul which, in its way, is profound in the extreme ; the soul now feels its natural darkness oppose the supernatural light, without feeling the supernatural light itself, for "the darkness does not comprehend it." Rather, it feels its natural darkness only is so far as it is penetrated by light, for no soul can see its own darkness except by the side of the Divine light until, the darkness being dissipated, itself becomes illumined and sees the light.

The flame lovingly and tenderly penetrates the will which comes to a knowledge of its own hardness and aridity when contrasted with God, though it does not feel the love and tenderness of the flame. . . . Each one suffers in proportion to his imperfections.

PERSEVERANCE IN LOVE

The constant practice of love is therefore a matter of all importance, so that the soul may become perfect therein, and may not be held back by the things of this world which keep it from drawing near to God.

THE BURNING TOUCH OF LOVE

But the soul is burned in another and most excellent way, which is this : when a soul is on fire with love . . . it will feel as if a seraph with a burning brand had struck it—already glowing as coal or rather all aflame—and had burnt it utterly. When the burning brand has thus touched it, the soul feels that the wound it has received is delicious beyond all imagination. . . . The soul feels, as it were, a most minute grain of mustard seed, most pungent and burning in the inmost heart of the spirit, diffuse itself most subtly through all spiritual veins. . . . The soul beholds itself now as one immense sea of fire.

Few souls attain to this state, but some have done so, especially those whose spirit and power are to be transmitted to their spiritual children ; for God freely bestows His gifts and graces on founders, and these in proportion to the importance of their teaching and the spirit which it is theirs to hand down. Thus it was with St. Francis, for when the seraph wounded his soul with love, the effects of that wound became outwardly visible. . . . God confers no favours on the body which He does not confer in the first place chiefly on the soul. . . . The greater the joy and violence of the love which is the cause of the interior wound, the greater will be the pain of the visible wound, and as the former grows so does the latter.

SUBSTANTIAL TOUCHES

We believe that this touch is most substantial, that the substance of God touches the substance of the soul. Many Saints have experienced it in this life. The sweetness of delight which this touch occasions baffles all description. But I will not speak of it, lest men should suppose that it is nothing beyond what my words imply; there are no terms by which we can designate or explain the deep things of God transacted in perfect souls. The proper way to speak of them is for him who has been favoured with them to understand them, feel them, and enjoy them, and be silent.

THE ABUNDANT GAIN OF THE SUBSTANTIAL TOUCHES

The touch, being of God, savoureth of everlasting life, and accordingly the soul tastes in a marvellous manner, and by participation, of all the things of God; fortitude, wisdom, love, beauty, grace, and goodness being communicated unto it.

Now as God is all this, the soul tastes of all in one single touch of God in a certain eminent way. And from this good bestowed upon the soul, some of the unction of the Spirit overflows at times into the body itself, penetrating into the very bones.

WHY FEW SOULS ATTAIN TO THE ESPOUSALS FEAR OF SUFFERING

Here comes the question, why is it that so few ever attain to this state ? . . . The reason is that, in this marvellous work which God Himself begins, so many are weak, shrinking from trouble, and unwilling to endure the least discomfort or mortification, or to labour with constant patience. Hence it is that God, not finding them diligent in cultivating the graces He has given them when He began to try them, proceeds no further with their purification, neither does He lift them up out of the dust of the earth, because it required greater courage and resolution for this than they possessed.

O souls that seek your own ease and comfort, if you knew how necessary for a high state is suffering, and how profitable suffering and mortification are for attaining to God's great blessings, you would never seek for comfort anywhere. . . . This is the way God deals with those whom it is His will to exalt : He suffers them to be tempted, afflicted, tormented and chastened, inwardly and outwardly, to the utmost limit of their strength, that He may deify them, unite them to Himself in His wisdom, which is the highest state.

DEATH TO HUMAN ACTIVITY

By that " death," of which the soul would speak, is meant the Old Man, that is, the employment of our faculties, memory, understanding and will upon the things of this world, and the desire and pleasure which created things supply. . . . All this is the old life.

As everything that lives, to use the expression of philosophers, lives in its acts, so the soul, having its acts in God by virtue of its union with Him, lives the life of God, its death being changed into life. . . . The understanding, which, previous to its union with God, understood but dimly by means of its natural light, is now under the influence and direction of another principle, and of a higher illumination of God. In this new life, when the soul shall have attained to perfect union with God, all its affections, powers and acts, in themselves imperfect and vile, become as it were divine.

In the same way, the will, which previously loved but weakly, is now changed into the life of divine love, for now it loves deeply with the affections of divine love, moved by the Holy Ghost in whom it now lives. The memory, which once saw nothing but the forms and figures of created things, is now changed, and " keeps in mind the eternal years," as David spoke. The desire, which previously longed for created food, now tastes and relishes the food that is divine, influenced by another and more efficacious principle, the sweetness of God.

Finally, all the motions and acts of the soul, proceeding from the principle of its natural and imperfect life, are now changed in this union with God into motions divine. For the soul, as the true child of God, is moved by the Spirit of God. . . . The substance of the soul, though it is not the substance of God, because inconvertible into Him, yet being united to Him and absorbed in Him, is by participation God.

THE CONDUCT OF CONTEMPLATIVE SOULS

In the first place, it is to be remembered that the caverns of the soul's powers are not conscious of their extreme emptiness when they are not purified and cleansed from all affection for created things. In this life every trifle that enters them is enough to perplex them, to render them insensible to their loss, and unable to recognise the infinite good which is wanting, or their own capacity for it. It is assuredly a most wonderful thing how, notwithstanding their capacity for infinite good, a mere trifle perplexes them, so that they cannot become the recipients of that for which they are intended till they are completely emptied.

But when they are empty and cleansed, the hunger, the thirst, and the anxiety of the spiritual sense become intolerable. This feeling of pain, so deep, usually occurs towards the close of the illumination and the purgation of the soul, previous to the state of perfect union, during which it is satisfied. For when the spiritual appetite is empty, pure from every creature and from every affection thereto, and when the natural temper is lost and the soul attempered to the divine, and the emptied appetite is well disposed—the divine communication in the union with God being still withheld—the pain of this emptiness and thirst is greater than that of death, especially then when certain glimpses of the divine ray are visible, but not communicated. Souls in this state suffer from impatient love, and they cannot endure it long without either receiving that which they desire, or dying.

The first cavern is the understanding; its emptiness is the thirst after God.

The second cavern is the will, and the emptiness thereof is a great hunger after God.

The third cavern is the memory, and the emptiness thereof is the soul's melting away and languishing for the possession of God.

It must be remembered above all that if a soul is seeking after God, the Beloved is seeking it much more.

The soul, therefore, considering that God is the chief doer in this matter, that it is He Who guides it and leads it by the hand whither it cannot come of itself, namely, unto supernatural things beyond the reach of understanding, memory, and will, must take especial care to put no difficulties in the way of its guide.

THE DIRECTOR SHOULD HAVE KNOWLEDGE AND EXPERIENCE

It is of the greatest importance to the soul desirous of perfection and anxious not to fall back, to consider well into whose hands it resigns itself; for as the master so is the disciple; as the father so the child. You will scarcely find one who is in all respects qualified to guide a soul in the higher parts of this road, or even in the ordinary divisions of it, for a director must be learned, prudent and experienced. Though the foundations of good direction be learning and discretion, yet if experience of the higher ways be wanting, there are no means of guiding a soul therein when God is showing the way, and inexperienced directors may do great harm. Such directors, not understanding the ways of the Spirit, very frequently make souls lose the unction of the delicate ointments, by means of which the Holy Ghost is preparing them for Himself: they are guiding them by other means of which they have read, but which are adapted only for beginners. These directors, knowing how to guide beginners only—and God grant they may know that—will not suffer their penitents to advance, though it be the will of God, beyond the mere rudiments, acts of reflection and imagination, whereby their progress is extremely little.

BEGINNERS: MEDITATION

In order to have a better knowledge of the state of beginners, we must keep in mind that it is one of meditation and of acts of reflection. It is necessary to furnish the soul in this state with matter for meditation, that it may make reflections and interior acts, and avail itself of sensible spiritual heat and fervour, for this is necessary in order to accustom the senses and desires to good things, that, being satisfied by the sweetness thereof, they may be detached from the world.

PASSAGE TO CONTEMPLATION

When this is in some degree effected, God begins at once to introduce the soul into the state of contemplation, and that very quickly, especially in religious, because these, having renounced the world, quickly fashion their senses and desires according to God;

they have therefore to pass at once from meditation to contemplation. This passage, then, takes place when the discursive acts and meditation fail, when sensible sweetness and first fervours cease, when the soul cannot make reflections as before, nor find any sensible comfort, but is fallen into aridity. . . . As all the natural operations of the soul, which are within its control, depend on the senses only, it follows that God is now working in a special manner in this state, that it is He that infuses and teaches, that the soul is the recipient on which He bestows spiritual blessings by contemplation. . . .

THE SOUL IS PASSIVE IN CONTEMPLATION

Souls in this state are not to be forced to meditate or to apply themselves to discursive reflections laboriously effected, neither are they to strive after sweetness and fervour, for if they did so, they would be thereby hindering the principal agent, Who is God Himself, for He is now secretly and quietly infusing wisdom into the soul, together with the loving knowledge of Himself, without many divers distinct or separated acts. But He produces them sometimes in the soul, and that for some space of time. The soul then must be lovingly intent upon God without distinctly eliciting other acts beyond these to which He inclines it; it must be as it were passive, making no efforts of its own, purely, simply and lovingly intent upon God, as a man who opens his eyes with loving attention.

For as God is now dealing with the soul in the way of bestowing by simple and loving knowledge, so the soul also, on its part, must deal with Him in the way of receiving by simple and loving knowledge, so that knowledge may be joined to knowledge, and love to love; because it is necessary here that the recipient should be adapted to the gift, and not otherwise, and that the gift may be accepted and preserved as it is given.

It is evident, therefore, that if the soul does not now abandon its ordinary way of meditation, it will receive this gift of God in a scanty and imperfect manner, not in that perfection with which it is bestowed; for the gift being so grand, and an infused gift, cannot be received in this scanty and imperfect way.

If the soul will at this time make efforts of its own, and encourage another disposition than that of passive loving attention, most submissive and calm, and if it does not abstain from its previous discursive acts, it will place a barrier against those graces which God is about to communicate to it in this loving knowledge.

But if the soul is to be the recipient of this loving knowledge, it must be perfectly detached, calm, peaceful, and serene, as God is; it must be like the atmosphere, which the sun illumines and warms in proportion to its calmness and purity. Thus the soul must be attached to nothing, not even to meditation, not to sensible or spiritual sweetness, because God requires a spirit free and annihilated, for every act of the soul, even of thought, of liking or disliking, will hinder and disturb it, and break that profound silence of sense and spirit necessary for hearing the deep and soft voice of God, Who speaks to the heart in solitude; it is in profound peace and tranquillity that the soul is to listen to God.

Therefore, under no circumstances whatever, either of time or place, is it lawful for the soul, now that it has begun to enter the state of contemplation, tranquil and simple, to recur to its previous meditation, or to cleave to spiritual sweetness. . . . It must detach itself from all spiritual sweetness, rise above it in freedom of spirit.

The soul must strive to root out all desire of consolation, sweetness, and meditations; not to disquiet itself about spiritual things, still less about earthly things; establish itself in perfect detachment, and in the utmost possible solitude. For the greater its progress in this, and the more rapidly it attains to this calm tranquillity, the more abundant will be the infusion of the spirit of divine wisdom, the loving, calm, lonely, peaceful, sweet ravisher of the spirit.

The interior goods which silent contemplation impresses on the soul without the soul's consciousness of them, are of inestimable value, for they are the most secret and delicious unctions of the Holy Ghost, whereby He secretly fills the soul with the riches of His gifts and graces. . . . What the soul is now conscious of is a certain estrangement and alienation from all things around it, at one time more than at another, with a certain sweet aspiration of love of the spirit, an inclination to solitude, and a sense of weariness in the things of this world, for when we taste of the spirit, the flesh becomes insipid.

THESE GOODS PENETRATE UNKNOWN TO THE SOUL AND TO ITS DIRECTOR

These goods, these great riches, neither the soul itself, nor he who directs it, can comprehend, but only He Who infuses them. They cannot under-stand these sublime and delicate unctions, this knowledge of the Holy Ghost, on account of their exquisite and subtle pureness.

THESE GOODS ARE EASILY LOST.
IGNORANT DIRECTORS

They are most easily disturbed and hindered, even by the slightest application of sense or desire to any particular knowledge or sweetness.

This is a serious evil, grievous and lamentable. Oh, how sad and how wonderful! The evil done is not perceived, and the barrier raised between God and the soul is almost nothing, and yet it is more grievous, an object of deeper sorrow, and inflicts a greater stain, than any other, though seemingly more important, in common souls which have not attained to such a high state of pureness.

Though this evil be so great that it cannot be exaggerated, it is still so common that there is scarcely one spiritual director who does not inflict it upon souls whom God has begun to lead by this way to contemplation. For, whenever God is anointing a soul with the unction of loving knowledge, most delicate, serene, peaceful, lonely, strange to sense and imagination; whenever He withholds all sweetness from it, and suspends its power of medita-tion—because He reserves it for this lonely unction, inclining it to solitude and quiet—a spiritual director will appear, who, like a rough blacksmith, knows only the use of his hammer, and who, because all his knowledge is limited to the coarser work, will say to it : Come, get rid of this, this is waste of time and idleness: arise and meditate, resume thy interior acts, for it is necessary that thou shouldest make diligent efforts of thine own; everything else is delusion and folly.

Such a director as this does not understand the degrees of prayer, nor the ways of the Spirit, neither does he consider that what he recommends the soul to do is already done; it has passed beyond meditation and is detached from the things of sense. . . . Such a director understands not that the soul has already attained to the life of the Spirit, wherein there is no reflection, and where the senses cease from their work; where God is Himself the agent in a special way, and is speaking in secret to the solitary soul.

The soul has already attained to the life of the Spirit, wherein there is no reflection, and where the senses cease from their work. To bring it back to the coarse ointments of particular knowledge and sensible sweetness, would be to rob it of its loneliness and recollection, and consequently disfigure the exquisite work which God was doing within it.

CONDUCT OF THE DIRECTOR

Let spiritual directors of this kind remember that the Holy Ghost is the principal agent here, and the real guide of souls; that He never ceases to take care of them and never neglects any means by which they may profit and draw near unto God as quickly as possible, and in the best way. Let them remember that they are not the agents, but instruments only to guide souls by the rule of the faith and the law of God, according to the spirit which God gives to everyone. Their aim therefore should be, not to

guide souls by a way of their own suitable to themselves, but to ascertain, if they can, the way by which
God Himself is guiding them. If they cannot
ascertain it, let them leave these souls alone and not
disquiet them.

Let them strive, therefore, to root out of the soul
all desire of consolation, sweetness, and meditations;
not disquiet it about spiritual things, still less about
earthly things; establish it in perfect detachment,
and in the utmost possible solitude.

The spiritual director must not be anxious or
afflicted because the soul is doing nothing, for God
is working in it. Provided the soul of his penitent
be detached from all particular knowledge, from
every desire and inclination of sense; provided it
abide in the self-denial of poverty of spirit. . . .
And this does not apply only to the renouncement
of temporal things, but of spiritual things for which
it must feel no ownership; for the Son of God
included poverty of spirit in the beatitudes. . . .
This is all that the soul should do, and all that the
spiritual director is to consider as within the province
of them both. It is impossible—according to the course
of the divine goodness and mercy—that God will not
perform His own work, yea, more impossible than that
the sun should not shine in a clear and cloudless sky.

As the sun rising in the morning enters the house
if the windows are open, so God . . . enters the
emptied soul and fills it with good things. God is,
like the sun, above our souls and ready to enter
within them.[1] . . . Let spiritual directors, therefore,

---

[1] "The beneficent light shines ceaselessly on all souls: it is ever
present, ever ready to give itself with divine liberality, ever ready
for souls to receive it."—DIONYSIUS: *Ecclesiastical Hierarchy*, III.

be content to prepare souls to receive His rays according to the laws of evangelical perfection, which consists in detachment, and in the emptiness of sense and spirit.

OBJECTION : IDLENESS ; EMPTINESS OF THE INTELLECT

Say not, therefore, that thy penitent is making no progress, or is doing nothing, for if he have no greater pleasure than he once had in particular knowledge, he is advancing towards that which is above nature. Neither do thou complain that thy penitent has no distinct perceptions, for if he had he would be making no progress, because God is incomprehensible, surpassing all understanding. And so the further the penitent advances, the further from himself must he go, walking by faith, believing and not seeing ; he thus draws nearer unto God by not understanding, than by understanding.[1]

For God, being incomprehensible, surpasses infinitely all the powers of human intelligence to understand Him. So the understanding, having neither the knowledge nor the power of comprehending God, advances towards Him by not

[1] " Then, delivered from the worlds of sense and of intellect, the soul enters into the mysterious darkness of holy ignorance, and renouncing all dealings with knowledge, it loses itself in Him Who can neither be seen nor apprehended ; it surrenders itself to this sovereign aim, no longer belonging to itself or to any other ; it is united to the unknown in the highest part of itself by reason of its renouncement of all knowledge ; and finally draws from this utter ignorance a knowledge that the understanding would never have been able to master."—DIONYSIUS : *Mystical Theology*, Chapter I., 3.

" For the very reason that it neither sees nor knows, it is truly united to Him Who surpasses all sight and all knowledge."—DIONYSIUS : *Letter to Dorothea*.

understanding, for if the understanding goes not backwards, occupying itself with distinct knowledge and other matters of this world, it is going forwards ; and to go forwards is to go more and more by faith. . . . Thus, then, what thou judgest amiss in thy penitent is for his profit : namely, that he does not perplex himself with distinct perceptions, but walks onwards in perfect faith.

LOVE WITHOUT DISTINCT KNOWLEDGE

Or, you will say, perhaps, that the will, if the understanding have no distinct perceptions, will be inevitably idle, and without love, because we can love nothing that we do not know. That is true as to the natural actions of the soul, for the will does not love or desire anything of which there is no distinct conception in the understanding.

But in the matter of contemplation, when God, as we have said, infuses something of Himself into the soul, it is not at all necessary for the soul to have distinct knowledge, or to form many discursive acts, because God Himself is then communicating to it loving knowledge, which is at the same time heat and light indistinctly. This is a supernatural knowledge of love, which lights and warms at the same time, because love is joined to the light. This light however remains dim and confused, for the knowledge belonging to contemplation is, according to Dionysius, a ray of darkness for the understanding. As the knowledge is general and dim—the understanding being unable to conceive distinctly what it understands—so the will also loves generally and indistinctly.

LOVE ALTERNATES WITH KNOWLEDGE

As God is light and love in this delicate communication, He informs equally the understanding and the will, though at times His presence is felt in one more than in the other. At one time the understanding is more filled with knowledge than the will with love, and, at another, love is deeper than knowledge.

God may separate the faculties and act in one whilst neglecting the other. He can enflame the will by the burning touch of His love, though the intellect may understand nothing of it, just as a person may feel the heat of a fire without being able to see it.

There is no reason, therefore, to be afraid of the will's idleness in this state, for if it ceases to elicit acts directed by particular knowledge, so far as they depend on itself, God inebriates it with infused love through the knowledge which contemplation ministers. . . . These acts of the will which are consequent upon infused contemplation are so much the nobler, the more meritorious and the sweeter, the nobler the source, God, Who infuses this love and kindles it in the soul, for the will is now near unto God, and detached from other joys.

Neither are we to be distressed when the memory is emptied of all forms and figures; for as God is without form or figure, the memory is safe when emptied of them, and draws thereby the nearer to God. For the more the memory relies on the imagination, the further it departs from God, and the greater the risks it runs; because God, being above our thoughts, is not cognisable by the imagination.

THE GREAT RESPONSIBILITY OF DIRECTORS

Some spiritual directors cannot understand souls who have already entered into the state of quiet and solitary contemplation, because they know it not, and perhaps have never advanced beyond the ordinary state of reflection and meditation themselves. Though such souls only desire to abide in quiet and peaceful self-recollection, such directors will have them strive after sweetness and fervours, though in truth they should have given them a wholly different advice.

Such directors as these do not really know what spirituality is. They wrong God most grievously, and treat Him irreverently, putting forth their coarse hands to the work which He is doing Himself. It has cost God not a little to have brought souls thus far, and He greatly prizes this solitude to which He has led them, this emptiness of their faculties, for He has brought them thither that He may speak to their heart, that is what He always desires.

It is not a light fault to cause by a wrong direction the loss of inestimable blessings, and to endanger a soul. Thus, he who rashly errs, being under an obligation to give good advice—for so is everyone in the office he assumes—shall not go unpunished for the evil he has done. The affairs of God are to be handled with great caution and watchful circumspection, and especially this, which is so delicate, and so high, and where the gain is infinite if the direction given be right, and the loss also infinite if it be wrong.

THE DEVIL

The other blind guide that disturbs the soul in this interior recollection is Satan, who, being blind himself, desires to render the soul blind also. He labours, therefore, when the soul has entered into those deep solitudes wherein the delicate unctions of the Holy Ghost are infused (he hates and envies the soul for this, because he sees it fly beyond his reach, adorned with the riches of God) to throw over the soul's detachment and estrangement from the world, he labours to give it certain . . . knowledge, and the darkness of sensible sweetness, sometimes good, the more to entice the soul, and to draw it back to the way of sense. He would have it fix its eyes on this, and make use of it with a view of drawing near to God, relying upon this kind of knowledge and sensible sweetness. By this means Satan distracts the soul, and easily withdraws it from that solitude and recollection wherein the Holy Ghost worketh secretly His great marvels within.

And then the soul, naturally prone to sensible satisfaction and sweetness—especially if it aims at them—is most easily led to rely upon such knowledge and sweetness, and so draws back from the solitude wherein God was working. For as the soul, as it seemed, was doing nothing then, this new way appears preferable, because it is something, while solitude seemed to be nothing. How sad it is that the soul, not understanding its own state, should, for one mouthful, disqualify itself for feeding upon God Himself; for He offers Himself to be its food when He absorbs it in these spiritual and solitary unctions of His mouth.

In this way, the evil spirit, for a mere nothing, inflicts upon souls the very greatest injuries, causing the loss of great riches, and dragging them forth, like fish with a trifling bait, out of the depths of the pure waters of the spirit, where they were engulfed and drowned in God, resting upon no created support. He drags them to the bank, and supplies them with objects whereon to rest, and makes them walk on the earth painfully, that they may not float on " the waters of Siloe, that run with silence," bathed in the unctions of God. It is wonderful how much Satan makes of this : and as a slight injury inflicted on the soul in this state is a great one, you will scarcely meet with one which has gone this way that has not suffered great injuries and incurred grievous losses. Satan stations himself with great cunning on the frontiers between sense and spirit ; there he deludes the soul, and feeds the senses, interposing sensible things to keep it back, and hinder it from escaping out of his hands.

If, therefore, a soul becomes recollected, he labours to disturb it by horrors and fears, or by bodily pains, or outward noise and tumults, that he may ruin it ; he strives to draw its attention to the tumult he excites, and to fix it upon what is passing without, and to withdraw it from the interior spirit, but when he fails in his efforts he leaves it alone.

HOW THE PASSIVE SOUL SHOULD BEHAVE

O souls, now that God shows you mercies so great, leading you into solitude and recollection, withdrawing you from the labours of sense, do not return thereto. If your own exertions were once profitable, enabling you to deny the world and your own selves when you were but beginners, cease from them now when God of His mercy has begun to work in you, for now they will only embarrass you. If you will be careful to lay no stress on your own operations, withdrawing them from all things, and involving them in nothing—which is your duty in your present state—and wait lovingly and sincerely upon God at the same time—doing no violence to yourselves except to detach yourselves wholly, so as not to disturb your tranquillity and peace—God Himself will feed you with the heavenly food, since you cease to hinder Him.

The soul itself, not understanding its own state, disturbs and injures itself. For as the soul knows of no operations except those of sense; when God leads it into solitude, where it cannot exert its faculties and elicit the acts it elicited before, and as it appears to itself then to be doing nothing, it strives to elicit its previous acts more distinctly and more sensibly. The consequence is distraction, dryness, and disgust in that very soul which once delighted in the calm peace and spiritual silence, wherein God Himself was in secret infusing His sweetness. It sometimes happens that God persists in keeping the soul in this quiet calm, and that the soul persists in crying out with the imagination, and in walking with the understanding.

The soul, then, should keep in mind that it is now making greater progress than it could make by any efforts of its own, though it be wholly unconscious of that progress. God Himself is carrying it in His own arms, and thus it happens that it is not aware that it is advancing. Though it thinks that it is doing nothing, yet in truth more is done than if itself were the agent; for God Himself is working. If this work be invisible, that is nothing strange, for the work of God in the soul is not cognisable by sense.

THE SENSE OF THE SOUL

The sense of the soul . . . is the power and energy of its very substance for perceiving and delighting in the objects of its spiritual faculties; the capacity thereof for possession, perception, and fruition; it is deep in proportion to the depth of the intelligence and love, and the communication of God.

THE AWAKENING OF THE BRIDEGROOM IN THE SOUL

In the awakening of the Bridegroom in the perfect soul, all is perfect because He effects it all Himself. . . . In this awakening, as of one aroused from sleep and drawing breath, the soul feels the breathing of God. . . . The Holy Ghost fills the soul with goodness and glory, whereby He inspires it with the love of Himself, transcending all glory and all understanding.

A SPIRITUAL CANTICLE OF THE SOUL AND THE BRIDEGROOM CHRIST

SONG OF THE SOUL AND THE BRIDEGROOM

THE BRIDE

Where hast Thou hidden Thyself,
And abandoned me in my groaning, O my Beloved
Thou hast fled like the hart,
Having wounded me.
I ran after Thee, crying; but Thou wert gone.

O shepherds, you who go
Through the sheepcots up the hill,
If you shall see Him
Whom I love the most,
Tell Him I languish, suffer, and die.

In search of my Love
I will go over mountains and strands;
I will gather no flowers,
I will fear no wild beasts;
And pass by the mighty and the frontiers.

O groves and thickets
Planted by the hand of the Beloved;
O verdant meads
Enamelled with flowers,
Tell me, has He passed by you?

ANSWER OF THE CREATURES

A thousand graces diffusing
He passed through the groves in haste,
And merely regarding them
As He passed
Clothed them with His beauty.

THE BRIDE

Oh! who can heal me?
Give me at once Thyself,
Send me no more
A messenger
Who cannot tell me what I wish.

All they who serve are telling me
Of Thy unnumbered graces;
And all wound me more and more,
And something leaves me dying,
I know not what, of which they are darkly speaking.

But how thou perseverest, O life,
Not living where thou livest;
The arrows bring death
Which thou receivest
From thy conceptions of the Beloved.

Why, after wounding
This heart, hast Thou not healed it?
And why, after stealing it,
Hast Thou thus abandoned it,
And not carried away the stolen prey?

Quench Thou my troubles,
For no one else can soothe them ;
And let mine eyes behold Thee,
For Thou art their light,
And I will keep them for Thee alone.

Reveal Thy presence,
And let the vision and Thy beauty kill me.
Behold the malady
Of love is incurable
Except in Thy presence and before Thy face.

O crystal well!
Oh that on Thy silvered surface
Thou wouldest mirror forth at once
Those eyes desired
Which are outlined in my heart!

Turn them away, O my Beloved!
I am on the wing :

THE BRIDEGROOM

Return, My Dove!
The wounded hart
Looms on the hill
In the air of thy flight and is refreshed.

THE BRIDE

My Beloved is the mountains,
The solitary wooded valleys,
The strange islands,
The roaring torrents,
The whisper of the amorous gales ;

The tranquil night
At the approaches of the dawn,
The silent music,
The murmuring solitude,
The supper which revives, and enkindles love.

Catch us the foxes,
For our vineyard hath flourished ;
While of roses
We make a nosegay,
And let no one appear on the hill.

O killing north wind, cease!
Come, south wind, that awakenest love!
Blow through my garden,
And let its odours flow,
And the Beloved shall feed among the flowers.

O nymphs of Judea!
While amid the flowers and the rose-trees
The amber sends forth its perfume,
Tarry in the suburbs,
And touch not our thresholds.

Hide thyself, O my Beloved!
Turn Thy face to the mountains.
Do not speak,
But regard the companions
Of her who is travelling amidst strange islands.

THE BRIDEGROOM

Light-wingèd birds,
Lions, fawns, bounding does,
Mountains, valleys, strands,
Waters, winds, heat,
And the terrors that keep watch by night ;

By the soft lyres
And the siren strains, I adjure you,
Let your fury cease,
And touch not the wall,
That the bride may sleep in greater security.

The bride has entered
The pleasant and desirable garden,
And there reposes to her heart's content ;
Her neck reclining
On the sweet arms of the Beloved.

Beneath the apple-tree
There wert thou betrothed ;
There I gave thee My hand,
And thou wert redeemed
Where thy mother was corrupted.

THE BRIDE

Our bed is of flowers
By dens of lions encompassed,
Hung with purple,
Made in peace,
And crowned with a thousand shields of gold.

In Thy footsteps
The young ones run Thy way ;
At the touch of the fire
And by the spiced wine,
The divine balsam flows.

In the inner cellar
Of my Beloved have I drunk ; and when I went forth
Over all the plain
I knew nothing,
And lost the flock I followed before.

There He gave me His breasts,
There He taught me the science full of sweetness.
And there I gave to Him
Myself without reserve ;
There I promised to be His bride.

My soul is occupied,
And all my substance in His service ;
Now I guard no flock,
Nor have I any other employment :
My sole occupation is love.

If, then, on the common land
I am no longer seen or found,
You will say that I am lost ;
That, being enamoured,
I lost myself ; and yet was found.

Of emeralds, and of flowers
In the early morning gathered,
We will make the garlands,
Flowering in Thy love,
And bound together with one hair of my head.

By that one hair
Thou hast observed fluttering on my neck,
And on my neck regarded,
Thou wert captivated;
And wounded by one of my eyes.

When Thou didst regard me,
Thine eyes imprinted in me Thy grace:
For this didst Thou love me again,
And thereby mine eyes did merit
To adore what in Thee they saw.

Despise me not,
For if I was swarthy once
Thou canst regard me now;
Since Thou hast regarded me,
Grace and beauty hast Thou given me.

THE BRIDEGROOM

The little white dove
Has returned to the ark with the bough;
And now the turtle-dove
Its desired mate
On the green banks has found.

In solitude she lived,
And in solitude built her nest;
And in solitude, alone
Hath the Beloved guided her,
In solitude also wounded with love.

THE BRIDE

Let us rejoice, O my Beloved!
Let us go forth to see ourselves in Thy beauty.
To the mountain and the hill,
Where the pure water flows :
Let us enter into the heart of the thicket.

We shall go at once
To the deep caverns of the rock
Which are all secret,
There we shall enter in
And taste of the new wine of the pomegranate.

There thou wilt show me
That which my soul desired ;
And there Thou wilt give at once,
O Thou, my life!
That which Thou gavest me the other day.

The breathing of the air,
The song of the sweet nightingale,
The grove and its beauty
In the serene night,
With the flame that consumes, and gives no pains.

None saw it ;
Neither did Aminadab appear.
The siege was intermitted,
And the cavalry dismounted
At the sight of the waters.

THE PURGATIVE WAY

THE TORMENT OF ABSENCE
DESIRE FOR UNION

Where hast Thou hidden Thyself,
And abandoned me in my groaning, O my beloved?
Thou hast fled like the hart,
Having wounded me.
I ran after Thee, crying; but Thou wert gone.

The soul, enamoured of the Word, the Son of God, the Bridegroom desiring to be united to Him in the clear and substantial vision, sets before Him the anxieties of its love, complaining of His absence. And this the more so because, now pierced and wounded with love, for which it had abandoned all things, even itself, it has still to endure the absence.

GOD IS HIDDEN WITHIN US

The Word, the Son of God, together with the Father and the Holy Ghost, is hidden in essence and in presence, in the inmost being of the soul. That soul, therefore, that will find Him, must go out from all things in will and affection, and enter into the profoundest self-recollection, and all things must be to it as if they existed not.

HOW TO SEEK GOD

Rest, therefore, neither wholly nor in part, on what thy faculties can embrace; never seek to satisfy thyself with what thou comprehendest of God, but rather with what thou comprehendest not; and never rest on the love of, and delight in, that which thou canst understand and feel, but rather on that which is beyond thy understanding and feeling. The less the soul understands distinctly, the nearer it is to God.

THE LANGUOR OF LOVE

O shepherds, you who go
Through the sheepcots up the hill,
If you shall see Him
Whom I love the most,
Tell Him I languish, suffer, and die.

The soul that truly loves God with a love in some degree perfect, suffers in three ways in His absence, in its three powers ordinarily—the understanding, the will, and the memory. In the understanding it languishes because it does not see God, Who is its salvation. . . . In the will it suffers, because it possesses not God, Who is its comfort and delight. . . . In the memory it dies, because it remembers its privation of all the blessings of the understanding, which are the vision of God, and of the delights of the will, which are the fruition of Him, and that it is very possible also that it may lose Him for ever, because of the dangers and chances of this life. In the memory, therefore, the soul labours under a sensation like that of death.

THE SOUL SHOWS ITS SUFFERINGS

Observe here that the soul does no more than represent its miseries and pain to the Beloved : for he who loves wisely does not care to ask for that which he wants and desires, being satisfied with hinting at his necessities, so that the Beloved One may do what shall to Him seem good. Thus the Blessed Virgin at the marriage feast of Cana asked not directly for wine. . . .

THE SOUL'S ACTIVITIES

In search of my Love
I will go over mountains and strands ;
I will gather no flowers,
I will fear no wild beasts ;
And pass by the mighty and the frontiers.

The soul, observing that its sighs and prayers suffice not to find the Beloved, and that it has not been helped by the messengers it invoked, will not leave undone anything that it can do of itself. The soul is now actively seeking the Beloved, in the practice of all virtue and in the spiritual exercises of the active and contemplative life ; for this end it rejects all delights and all comforts ; and all the power and wiles of its three enemies, the world, the devil, and the flesh, are unable to delay it or hinder it on the road.

He who seeks God, consulting his own ease and

comfort, seeks Him by night, and therefore finds Him not. But he who seeks Him in the practice of virtue and of good works, casting aside the comforts of his own bed, seeks Him by day; such a one shall find Him, for that which is not seen by night is visible by day.

DESIRE FOR THE FULL POSSESSION OF GOD

> Oh! who can heal me ?
> Give me at once Thyself,
> Send me no more
> A messenger
> Who cannot tell me what I wish.

The soil says : " Entertain me no more with any knowledge or communications or impressions of Thy grandeur, for these do but increase my longing and the pain of Thy absence ; Thy presence alone can satisfy my will and desire." The will cannot be satisfied with anything less than the vision of God, and therefore the soul prays that He may be pleased to give Himself to it in truth, in perfect love. . . . " O Lord my Bridegroom, Who didst give me Thyself partially before, give me Thyself wholly now."

" Grant that I may no longer know Thee in this imperfect way by the messengers of knowledge and impressions, which are so distant from that which my soul desires ; for these messengers, as Thou well knowest, O my Bridegroom, do but increase the pain of Thy absence. They renew the wound which Thou has inflicted by the knowledge of Thee which they convey, and they seem to delay Thy coming.

Henceforth do Thou send me no more of these inadequate communications, for if I have been hitherto satisfied with them, it was owing to the slightness of my knowledge and of my love; now that my love has become great, I cannot satisfy myself with them; do Thou, therefore, give me at once Thyself. . . . Instead of these messengers, therefore, be Thou the messenger and the message Thyself."

THE AGONY OF THE SOUL

All they who serve are telling me
Of Thy unnumbered graces;
And all wound me more and more,
And something leaves me dying,
I know not what, of which they are darkly speaking.

The pain is like dying. . . . The soul is dying a living death until love, having slain it, shall make it live the life of love, transforming it in love. This dying of love is affected by a single touch of the knowledge of the Divinity. . . . This touch is not continuous nor great—for then soul and body would part—but soon over, and thus the soul is dying of love, and dying the more when it sees that it cannot die of love.

THE INFINITE IS INCOMPREHENSIBLE

The impression of this dying is given occasionally to souls advanced, whom God favours in what they hear, or see, or understand—with a certain profound knowledge, in which they feel or apprehend the greatness and majesty of God. In this state they think so highly of God as to see clearly that they know Him not, and in their perception of His greatness they recognise that not to comprehend Him is the highest comprehension. And thus, one of the greatest favours of God, bestowed transiently on the soul in this life, is to enable it to see so distinctly, and to feel so profoundly, that it clearly understands it cannot comprehend Him at all.

THE SIGNS THAT GOD HAS TAKEN POSSESSION OF THE SOUL

> Why, after wounding
> This heart, hast Thou not healed it ?
> And why, after stealing it,
> Hast Thou thus abandoned it,
> And not carried away the stolen prey ?

Whether God has really stolen the heart, the soul may ascertain by either of these two signs : Is it anxiously seeking after God ? and has it no pleasure in anything but in Him, as the soul here says ? The heart cannot rest in peace without the possession of something ; and when its affections are once placed, it has neither the possession of itself nor of anything else ; neither does it perfectly possess what it loves. In this state its weariness is in proportion to its loss, until it shall enter into possession and be satisfied ; for until then the soul is as an empty vessel waiting to be filled, as a hungry man eager for food, as a sick man sighing for health, and as a man suspended in the air without support to his feet.

THE SOUL WOUNDED BY DIVINE LOVE

The soul in pain because of its love of God, has three marks which show its state. Under all circumstances, and in all affairs, the thought of its health—that is, the Beloved—is ever present to it; and though it is obliged to attend to material occupations because it cannot help it, its heart is ever with Him. The second mark, namely, a loss of pleasure in everything, arises from the first. The third also, a consequence of the second, is that all things become wearisome, and all affairs full of vexation and annoyance.

Souls thus in love suffer greatly in their intercourse with men and in the transactions of the world, because these things hinder rather than help them in their search.

The source of the grievous sufferings of the soul at this time is the consciousness of its own emptiness of God—while it is drawing nearer and nearer to Him. In the midst of darkness it is tormented by spiritual fire, which dries and purifies it, that it may be united with God. For when God sends not forth a ray of supernatural light into the soul, He is to it intolerable darkness even when He is near to it in spirit, for the supernatural light by its very brightness obscures the mere natural light.

II

THE ILLUMINATIVE WAY

§ THE SPIRITUAL BETROTHAL
ECSTASIES

Turn them away, O my Beloved!
I am on the wing :

As the soul has so anxiously prayed, the Beloved
reveals to it some glimpses of His majesty and God-
head, according to its desires. These divine rays
strike the soul so profoundly and so vividly that it
is rapt into an ecstasy which in the beginning is
attended with great suffering and natural fear.

So great, at times, is the suffering of the soul
during these ecstatic visitations—and there is no
other pain which so wrenches the very bones, and
which so oppresses our natural forces—that, were it
not for the special interference of God, death would
ensue. And, in truth, such is it to the soul, the
subject of these visitations, for it feels as if it were
released from the body and a stranger to the flesh.
They who are already perfect receive these visitations in peace and in the sweetness of love : ecstasies
cease, for they were only graces to prepare them for
this greater grace.

THE SPIRITUAL BETROTHAL

My Beloved is the mountains,
The solitary wooded valleys,
The strange islands,

The roaring torrents,
The whisper of the amorous gales;

The tranquil night
At the approaches of the dawn,
The silent music,
The murmuring solitude,
The supper which revives, and enkindles love.

The spiritual flight signifies a certain high estate and union of love, whereunto, after many spiritual exercises, God is wont to elevate the soul: it is called the spiritual betrothal of the Word, the Son of God. In the beginning, when this occurs the first time, God reveals to the soul great things of Himself, makes it beautiful in majesty and grandeur. . . . On this happy day the soul not only ceases from its anxieties and loving complaints, but, is moreover, adorned with all grace, entering into a state of peace and delight, a state of sweet and peaceful intercourse of love with the Beloved.

In this divine union the soul has a vision and foretaste of abundant and inestimable riches, and finds there all the repose and refreshment it desired; it attains to the secrets of God, and to a strange knowledge of Him, which is the food of those who know Him most; it is conscious of the awful power of God beyond all other power and might, tastes of the wonderful sweetness and delight of the Spirit, finds its true rest and divine light, drinks deeply of the wisdom of God, which shines forth in the harmony of the creatures, and the works of God; it feels itself filled with all good, emptied, and delivered from all evil, and, above all, rejoices consciously in the inestimable banquet of love which confirms it in love.

THE SOUL FINDS AND EXPERIENCES THAT GOD IS ALL

We are not to understand this consciousness of the soul as if it saw creatures in God as we see material objects in the light, but that in possessing God, the soul knows He is all things; neither are we to imagine that the soul sees God essentially and clearly because it has so deep a sense of Him; for this is only a strong and abundant communication from Him, a glimmering light of what He is in Himself, by which the soul discerns this goodness of all things.

THE KNOWLEDGE IS STILL DARK

This most subtle and delicate knowledge enters with marvellous sweetness and delight into the inmost substance of the soul, which is the highest of all delights.

The reason is that substantial knowledge is now communicated intelligibly, and stripped of all accidents and images, to the understanding—which philosophers call passive or passible, because inactive without any natural efforts of its own. . . . This is the highest delight of the soul, because it is in the understanding, which is the seat of fruition, as theologians teach, and fruition is the vision of God.

Still, we are not to think that what the soul perceives, though pure truth, can be the perfect and

clear fruition of Heaven. For though it be free
from accidents, it is dim and not clear, because
it is contemplation, which in this life, as St.
Dionysius saith, "is a ray of darkness," and thus
we may say that it is a ray and an image of
fruition, because it is in the understanding, which
is the seat of fruition.

THE DAWN OF A NEW KNOWLEDGE

This tranquillity and repose in God is not all
darkness to the soul, as the dark night is, but rather
tranquillity and repose in the divine light and in a
new knowledge of God, whereby the mind, most
sweetly tranquil, is raised to a divine light. . . .
This divine light is called the approaches of the
dawn. . . . The mind, tranquil and reposing in God,
is raised up from the darkness of natural knowledge
to the morning light of the supernatural knowledge
of God; not clear, indeed, as I have said, but dim,
like the night at the approaches of the dawn. For
as it is then neither wholly night nor wholly day,
but, as they say, twilight. . . . In this tranquillity
the understanding is lifted up in a strange way above
its natural comprehension to the divine light. . . .
In the same way, in this tranquil contemplation, the
soul beholds all creatures, each one magnifying God
in its own way, and possessing Him according to its
particular capacity.

THE SOUL HAS NOT YET PERFECT PEACE

In the state of betrothal, wherein the soul enjoys
tranquillity, and wherein it receives all that it can

receive in this life, we are not to suppose its tranquillity to be perfect, but that the higher part of it is tranquil; for the sensual part, except in the state of spiritual marriage, never loses all its imperfect habits, and its powers are never wholly subdued, as I shall show hereafter. What the soul receives now is all that it can receive in the state of betrothal, for in that of the marriage the blessings are greater. Though the bride-soul has great joy in these visits of the Beloved in the state of betrothal, still it has to suffer from His absence, to endure trouble and afflictions in the lower part, and at the hands of the devil. But all this ceases in the state of spiritual marriage.

TROUBLES CAUSED BY THE DEVIL

The devil, beholding the prosperity of the soul, and in his great malice envying all the good he sees in it, now uses all his power, and has recourse to all his devices, in order to thwart it, if possible, even in the slightest degree. He thinks it of more consequence to keep back the soul, even for an instant, from this abundance, bliss, and delight, than to make others fall into many and mortal sins.

The devil has recourse to the sensual appetites, though now they can give him generally but little or no help, because they are mortified, and because he cannot turn them to any great account in distracting the imagination. Sometimes he stirs up many movements in the sensitive part of the soul, and causes other vexations, spiritual as well as sensual, from which the soul is unable to deliver itself.

Catch us the foxes,
For our vineyard hath flourished ;
While of roses
We make a nosegay,
And let no one appear on the hill.

The evil spirits now molest the soul in two ways. They vehemently excite the desires, and employ them with other imaginations to assail the peaceful and flourishing kingdom of the soul. Then—and this is much worse—when they do not succeed in stirring up the desires, they assail the soul with bodily pains and noises in order to distract it. And, what is still more serious, they fight with spiritual horror and dread, and sometimes with fearful torments, which, at this time, if God permits them, they can most effectually bring about, for inasmuch as the soul is now spiritually detached, so as to perform its spiritual exercises, the devil being himself a spirit presents himself before it with great ease.

The devil knows well that once entered into this state of recollection it is there so protected that, notwithstanding all he can do, he cannot hurt it. Very often, too, when the devil goes forth to meet the soul, the soul becomes quickly recollected in the secret depths of its interior, where it finds great sweetness and protection ; then those terrors of Satan are so far off that they not only produce no fear, but are even the occasion of peace and joy.

DESIRE FOR DETACHMENT FROM THE SENSES

The soul prays to the Angels that no representation or image of any object whatever appertaining to any of its faculties or senses may be interposed between itself and its Bridegroom. . . . In other words, that the spiritual powers of the soul, memory, understanding, and will, may be divested of all notions, particular inclinations, or considerations whatsoever.

The soul speaks in this way because it is necessary for the perfect fruition of this communication of God, that all the senses and powers, both interior and exterior, should be disencumbered and emptied of their proper objects and operations; for the more active they are, the greater will be the hindrance which they will occasion. The soul having attained to a certain interior union of love, the spiritual faculties of it are no longer active, and still less those of the body; for now that the union of love is actually wrought in love, the faculties of the soul cease from their exertions, because now that the goal is reached all employment of means is at an end. What the soul at this time has to do is to wait lovingly upon God, and this waiting is love in a continuation of unitive love.

THE SUFFERING THAT COMES FROM CLEARER KNOWLEDGE

O killing north wind, cease!
Come, south wind, that awakenest love!
Blow through my garden,

And let its odours flow,
And the Beloved shall feed among the flowers.

In the state of spiritual espousals the soul contem-
plating its great riches and excellence, but unable to
enter into the possession and fruition of them as it
desires, because it is still in the flesh, often suffers
exceedingly, and then more particularly when its
knowledge of them becomes more profound.

LONGING FOR SUBSTANTIAL CONTACT

Hide Thyself, O my Beloved!
Turn thy face to the mountains.
Do not speak
But regard the companions
Of her who is travelling amidst strange islands.

The soul prays to see the face of God, which is
the essential communication of His Divinity to the
soul, without any intervening medium, by a certain
knowledge thereof in the Divinity. This is something beyond sense, and divested of accidents,
inasmuch as it is the contact of pure substances—
that is, of the soul and the Divinity.

It adds, " Do not speak."

That is, do not speak as before, when Thy converse with me was known to the outward senses, for
it was once such as to be comprehended by them ;
it was not so profound but they could fathom it.
Now let Thy converse with me be so deep and so
substantial, and so interior, as to be above the reach
of the senses ; for the substance of the spirit is
incommunicable to sense, and the communication

made through the senses, especially in this life, cannot be purely spiritual, because the senses are not capable of it. The soul, therefore, longing for that substantial and essential communication of God, of which sense cannot be cognisant, prays the Bridegroom not to speak : that is to say, let the deep secret of the spiritual union be such as to escape the notice of the senses, like the secret which St. Paul heard, and which it is not lawful for a man to speak.

THE STRENGTH OF THE SOUL

In this state the soul not only attains to exceeding pureness and beauty, but also acquires a terrible strength by reason of that strict and close bond which in this union binds it to God.

ANGELIC IMPASSIBILITY OF THE SOUL

Light-wingèd birds,
Lions, fawns, bounding does,
Mountains, valleys, strands,
Waters, winds, heat,
And the terrors that keep watch by night ;

By the soft lyres
And the siren strains, I adjure you,
Let your fury cease,
And touch not the wall,
That the bride may sleep in greater security.

Such is the grandeur and stability of the soul in this state, that, although formerly the waters of grief overwhelmed it, because of its own or other men's sins—which is what spiritual persons most feel—the consideration of them now excites neither pain nor annoyance; even the sensible pain of contrition exists not now, though the effects of it continue in perfection. The weaknesses of its virtues are no longer in the soul, for they are now constant, strong, and perfect. As the angels perfectly appreciate all sorrowful things without the sense of pain, and perform acts of mercy without the sentiment of pity, so the soul in this transformation of love. God, however, makes exceptions in this matter on certain occasions, allowing the soul to feel and suffer, that it may become more fervent in love, and grow in merit, or for some other reasons, as He acted thus with His Virgin Mother, St. Paul, and others. This, however, is not the ordinary condition of this state.

PEACE AND PLENITUDE

The desires of hope do not afflict the soul now, because, satisfied in its union with God, so far as it is possible in this life, it has nothing of this world to hope for, and nothing spiritual to desire. It feels itself full of the riches of God, whether it is living or dying, it is conformed to the will of God, saying with the sense and spirit, " Thy will be done ", it is free from the violence of inclination and desires.

THE LIGHT OF GLORY

God sometimes produces within the soul a certain spiritual communion wherein He causes it to behold and enjoy at the same time the abyss of delight and riches which He has laid up within it.

THE PRIVILEGES OF THE BRIDE

The soul has it now in its power to abandon itself whenever it wills to this sweet sleep of love.

III

THE UNITIVE WAY

§ THE SPIRITUAL MARRIAGE

The bride has entered
The pleasant and desirable garden,
And there reposes to her heart's content;
Her neck reclining
On the sweet arms of the Beloved.

This is, beyond all comparison, a far higher state than that of betrothal, because it is a complete transformation into the Beloved; whereby they surrender each to the other the entire possession of themselves in the perfect union of love, wherein the soul becomes divine, and, by participation, God, so far as it is possible in this life. I believe that no soul ever attains to this state without being confirmed in grace, for the faithfulness of both is confirmed; that of God being confirmed in the soul.[1]

The soul has entered this state because it has detached itself from all temporal and natural things, from all spiritual affections, ways, and methods, having left on one side, and forgotten, all temptations, trials, sorrows, anxieties and cares, transformed in this embrace of God.

When the soul has lived for some time as the bride of the Son, in perfect and sweet love, God calls it and leads it into His flourishing garden for the

[1] Human marriage: et erunt in *carne una* (S. Matt. xix.)
Spiritual marriage: Qui autem adhaeret Domino, *unus spiritus* est (1 Cor. vi. 17).

celebration of the spiritual marriage. Then the two natures are so united, what is divine is so communicated to what is human, that, without undergoing any essential change, each seems to be God— yet not perfectly so in this life, though still in a manner which can neither be described nor conceived.

THE BRIDEGROOM REVEALS HIS SECRETS TO THE BRIDE

The chief matter of His communications are the sweet mysteries of His incarnation, the ways and means of redemption, which is one of the highest works of God, and so is to the soul one of the sweetest.

THE STRENGTH OF THIS SOUL

Our bed is of flowers
By dens of lions encompassed,
Hung with purple,
Made in peace,
And crowned with a thousand shields of gold.

The soul also, united to Him in those very virtues, is as a strong lion, because it then partakes of the perfections of God.

The perfect soul is so defended, so strong in virtue, and in all virtues together, reposing on the flowery bed of its union with God, that the evil spirits are not only afraid to assault it, but even dare not appear before it ; such is their dread of it, when they behold it strong, courageous, and mature in its perfect virtues, on the bed of the Beloved. The evil spirits fear a soul transformed in the union of love as much as they fear the Beloved Himself, and they dare not look upon it, for Satan is in great fear of that soul which has attained to perfection.

The soul being now free from all molestation of natural affections, and a stranger to the worry of temporal anxieties, enjoys in security and peace the participation of God.

LOVE DOES NOT DEPEND ON KNOWLEDGE

In the inner cellar
Of my Beloved have I drunk; and when I went forth
Over all the plain
I knew nothing,
And lost the flock I followed before.

There is a common saying that the will cannot love that of which the understanding has no knowledge. This, however, is to be understood in the order of nature, it being impossible, in a natural way, to love anything unless we first know what it is we love. But in a supernatural way God can certainly infuse love and increase it without infusing and increasing distinct knowledge, as is evident from the texts already quoted. Yea, many spiritual persons have experience of this; their love of God burns more and more, while their knowledge does not grow. Men may know little and love much, and, on the other hand, know much and love but little.

In general, those spiritual persons whose knowledge of God is not very great are usually very rich in all that belongs to the will, and infused faith suffices them for this knowledge, by means of which God infuses and increases charity in them and the acts thereof, which are to love Him more and more though knowledge is not increased. Thus the will may drink of love while the understanding drinks in no fresh knowledge.

THE SOUL IS INEBRIATED WITH LOVE

The soul is now, in a certain sense, like Adam in paradise, who knew no evil. It is so innocent that it sees no evil; neither does it consider anything to be amiss. It will hear much that is evil, and will see it with its eyes, and yet it shall not be able to understand it, because it has no evil habits whereby to judge of it. God has rooted out of it those imperfect habits and that ignorance resulting from the evil of sin, by the perfect habit of true wisdom. Thus, also, the soul knows nothing on this subject.

Such a soul will scarcely intermeddle with the affairs of others, because it forgets even its own; for the work of the Spirit of God in the soul in which He dwells is to incline it to ignore those things which do not concern it, especially such as do not minister to edification. The Spirit of God abides within the soul to withdraw it from outward things rather than to lead it among them; and thus the soul knows nothing as it knew it formerly. We are not, however, to suppose that it loses the habits of knowledge previously acquired, for those habits are improved by the more perfect habit of supernatural knowledge infused, though these habits be not so powerful as to necessitate knowledge through them, and yet there is no reason why they should not do so occasionally.

In this union of the divine wisdom these habits are united with the higher wisdom of other knowledge, as a little light with another which is great; it is the great light that shines, overwhelming the less, yet the latter is not therefore lost, but rather perfected, though it be not the light which shines pre-eminently.

But the particular notions and forms of things, acts of the imagination, and every other apprehension having form and figure, are all lost and ignored in this absorbing love, and this for two reasons. First, the soul cannot actually attend to anything of the kind, because it is actually absorbed by this draught of love. Secondly, and this is the principal reason, its transformation in God so conforms it to His purity and simplicity—for there is no form or imaginary figure in Him—as to render it pure, cleansed and empty of all the forms and figures it entertained before, being now purified and enlightened in simple contemplation. All spots and stains in the glass become invisible when the sun shines upon it, but they appear again as soon as the light of the sun is withheld.

So is it with the soul; while the effects of this act of love continue, this ignorance continues also, so that it cannot observe anything in particular until these effects have ceased. Love has set the soul on fire and transmuted it into love, has annihilated it and destroyed it as to all that is not love, according to the words of David: "My heart hath been inflamed, and my reins have been changed; and I am brought to nothing, and I knew not."[1]

[1] Ps. lxxii. 21, 22.

ONLY LOVE CAN MAKE THE SOUL PLEASING TO GOD

> My soul is occupied,
> And all my substance in His service;
> Now I guard no flock,
> Nor have I any other employment:
> My sole occupation is love.

God is pleased with nothing but love. . . . All our works, and all our labours, how grand soever they may be, are nothing in the sight of God, for we can give Him nothing, neither can we by them fulfil His desire, which is the growth of our soul. . . . As there is no way in which the soul can grow but in becoming in a manner equal to Him, for this reason only is He pleased with our love. It is the property of love to place him who loves on an equality with the object of his love. Hence the soul, because of its perfect love, is called the bride of the Son of God, which signifies equality with Him. In this equality and friendship all things are common.

THE SOUL IS CENTRED IN LOVE

The soul surrenders itself to the Beloved in this union of love, wherein it devotes itself, with all its faculties, understanding, will, and memory, to His service.

The understanding is occupied in considering what most tends to His service, in order that it might be accomplished; the will in loving all that is pleasing to God, and in desiring Him in all things; the memory in recalling what ministers to Him, and what may be more pleasing unto Him.

When the soul has arrived at this state of prayer
he acts of its spiritual and sensual nature, whether
active or passive, and of whatever kind they may be,
always occasion an increase of love and delight in
God : even the act of prayer and communion with
God, which was once carried on by reflections and
divers other methods, is now wholly an act of love.
So much so is this the case that the soul may always
say, whether occupied with temporal or spiritual
things, " My sole occupation is love."

§ THE CONTEMPLATIVE LIFE

(St. Mary Magdalene)

If, then, on the common land
I am no longer seen or found,
You will say that I am lost ;
That, being enamoured,
I lost myself ; and yet was found.

So precious is the contemplative life in the eyes
of God that He rebuked Martha because she would
withdraw Mary from His feet to occupy her actively
in the service of our Lord. Martha thought that
she was doing everything herself, and that Mary at
the feet of Christ was doing nothing. But it was
far otherwise : for there is nothing better or more
necessary than love.

Observe, however, that if the soul has not reached
the state of unitive love, it is necessary for it to make
acts of love, as well in the active as in the contemplative life. But when it has reached it, it is not
requisite it should occupy itself in other and exterior

duties—unless they be matters of obligation—which
might hinder, were it but for a moment, the life o
love in God, though they may minister greatly t
His service; because an instant of pure love is mor
precious in the eyes of God and the soul, and mor
profitable to the Church, than all other good work
together, though it may seem as if nothing wer
done. Thus, Mary Magdalene, though her preach
ing was most edifying, and might have been sti
more so afterwards, out of the great desire she ha
to please God and benefit the Church, hid hersel
nevertheless, in the desert thirty years, that sh
might surrender herself entirely to love; for sh
considered that she would gain more in that way
because an instant of pure love is so much mor
profitable and important to the Church.

When the soul, then, in any degree possesses th
spirit of solitary love, we must not interfere with i
We should inflict a grievous wrong upon it, an
upon the Church also, if we were to occupy it, wer
it only for a moment, in exterior or active dutie
however important they might be.

ACTIVITY IS VAIN WITHOUT CONTEMPLATION

In a word, it is for this love that we are all create
Let those men of zeal, who think by their preachin
and exterior works to convert the world, conside
that they would be much more edifying to th
Church, and more pleasing unto God—setting asid
the good example they would give—if they woul
spend at least one-half their time in prayer, eve
though they may have not attained to the state c
unitive love. Certainly they would do more, an

with less trouble, by one single good work than by a thousand : because of the merit of their prayer, and the spiritual strength it supplies. To act otherwise is to beat the air, to do little more than nothing, sometimes nothing and occasionally even mischief ; for God may give up such persons to vanity, so that they may seem to have done something, when in reality their outward occupations bear no fruit ; for it is quite certain that good works cannot be done but in the power of God.

GOD IS GAINED BY POVERTY OF SPIRIT

When a soul has advanced so far on the spiritual road as to be lost to all the natural methods of communing with God ; when it seeks Him no longer by meditations, images, impressions, nor by any other created ways, or representations of sense, but only by rising above them all, in the joyful communion with Him by faith and love, then it may be said to have found God of a truth, because it has truly lost itself as to all that is not God, and also as to its own self.

ALONE WITH GOD IN PERFECT SOLITUDE

In solitude she lived,
And in solitude built her nest ;
And in solitude, alone
Hath the Beloved guided her,
In solitude also wounded with love.

The Beloved not only guides the soul in its solitude, but it is He alone Who works in it directly and immediately. It is of the nature of the soul's union with God in the spiritual marriage that God works directly, and communicates Himself immediately, not by the ministry of angels or by the help of natural capacities. For the exterior and interior senses, all created things, and even the soul itself, contribute very little towards the reception of those great supernatural favours which God bestows in this state; yea, rather, inasmuch as they do not fall within the cognisance of natural efforts, ability and application, God effects them alone.

The reason is, that He finds the soul alone in its solitude, and therefore will not give it another companion, nor will He entrust His work to any other than Himself.

THE NECESSITY OF SUFFERING

Let us rejoice, O my Beloved!
Let us go forth to see ourselves in Thy beauty.
To the mountain and the hill,
Where the pure water flows:
Let us enter into the heart of the thicket.

O that men would understand how impossible it is to enter the thicket, the manifold riches of the wisdom of God, without entering into the thicket of manifold suffering, making it the desire and consolation of the soul; and how that the soul which really longs for the divine wisdom longs first of all for the sufferings of the Cross.